What's in Your Glass?

Pentecostal Christians, Sugary Drinks, and Their Dangers

Eric Tangumonkem, Ph.D.

IEM PRESS (PO Box 831001, Richardson, TX 75080) functions only as a book publisher. As such, the ultimate design, content, editorial accuracy, and views expressed or implied in this work are those of the author. No part of this publication may be reproduced, stored in a retrieval system, or transmitted in any way by any means—electronic, mechanical, photocopy, recording, or otherwise—without the prior permission of the copyright holder, except as provided by USA copyright law. Unless otherwise noted, all Scriptures are taken from the Holy Bible, New International Version®, NIV®. Copyright © 1973, 1978, 1984, 2011 by Biblica, Inc.™ Used by permission of Zondervan. All rights reserved worldwide. www. zondervan.com
ISBN

ISBN 13: 978-1-63603-009-8

Library of Congress Catalog Card Number: 2020945938

Dedication:

To my wife, Elizabeth Tayem, for her "Sugar Sucks" campaign and working tirelessly to bring awareness to the dangers of consuming processed sugar.

#sugarsucks #sugarisakiller

Table of Contents

Introduction 1

Chapter 1: Why I wrote this book 5

Chapter 2: True confession.. 11

Chapter 3: Jesus Christ turned water into
wine 23

Chapter 4: The inconvenient truth about
sugar.. 55

Chapter 5: The devil is in the details!..................... 81

Chapter 6: It is not a sin not to drink sugary
drinks.. 91

Chapter 7: An eternal perspective is the
ultimate one... 111

Acknowledgement... 123

About the Author... 125

Other Resources by the Author 127

Introduction

How can something sweet be bad for your health? This is a legitimate question that many people have. In this book, I am going to be taking a close look at sugar and how it has made a stronghold in the lives of many.

I am not attempting to against sugary drinks or artificial sugars, it is a wakeup call to those who believe that if a drink is sweet and non-alcoholic, it must not be bad. I may be oversimplifying it, but this book is going to be a critical look at the teachings that I was raised in, and the far-reaching implications of the wholesale embrace, without reservation, of sugary drinks.

Most fervent Pentecostal believers do not drink or touch any alcohol. Instead, they focus on being filled with the Holy Spirit. They take this matter seriously and do not compromise. This belief has led many people to start drinking sugary drinks to replace alcohol. They assume that since these drinks are non-alcoholic, they are safe to consume because they won't get drunk, but in reality, this practice is even more problematic.

What has kept this problem in the dark is the fact that the Bible never mentions if we should drink soda pop or not. To look for solutions to this problem, we are going to look deeper into scripture.

This book will not dwell on the question of whether the followers of Jesus Christ should or shouldn't drink alcoholic drinks. That is a discussion outside the scope of this book. The focus of this book is going to be on non-alcoholic sugary beverages. The book will be highlighting the dangers of drinking sugar and the long-term health hazards associated with it.

Just because a drink is sweet and cannot make you drunk does not mean that it is good for your health. The danger posed by sugar-loaded drinks is real and must be taken seriously. Many are quick to dismiss this warning because the effects of alcoholic beverages can be seen immediately. But sugary drinks can get a pass because their impact is slow and not so easily noticed.

When you ask people who are suffering from type-2 diabetes, obesity, chronic fatigue, cognitive challenges, insomnia, and other health issues, you will see how harmful sugar can be. Some people have gone as far as labeling processed sugar a poison, and rightfully so.

The hope is that when you are done reading this book, you will be able to understand the connection between alcoholic and non-alcoholic beverages. The argument that Jesus turned water into wine is brought up by both sides. But is the wine that Jesus made the same as soda pop? This question will be answered in chapter three. In addition to that, we will be dwelling on the implications of equating soda pop and all the modern-day sugar-loaded drinks to the wine that Jesus made.

A considerable amount of effort is made in chapter four to bring forth the dangers of processed sugar. This is because the sugar in non-alcoholic drinks, in most cases, is artificially processed sugar. The drawbacks of this processed sugar, especially fructose corn syrup, are enormous. Therefore, anybody who wants to live a healthy life should avoid processed sugar as much as possible. If you can drink water most of the time, your body will be much healthier.

The other thing that the book focuses on is the content of these sugary drinks. Many people do not pay attention to the labels on the bottles. In some countries, the drink makers are not required to disclose any information on what is found in the drink. Therefore, people are clueless about what they are putting into their bodies. The hope is that exposing people to what is actually in the drinks will help them make a more informed decision on whether or not they should drink them; this will be the main topic in chapter five.

Chapter six poses the question: is it a sin to drink sugar-loaded drinks or not? While this question can be very straight forward, the answer is no. But we are going to draw inspiration from scripture to better understand this crucial question.

There is more to living a healthy and productive life on Earth than just avoiding sugary drinks. You must think about eternal life as well. This implies that you need to also focus on what truly matters: the state of your spiritual life. The last chapter of this book will allow you to make things right with God if you have not already done so. I hope you will take advantage of this offer. Happy reading!

Chapter 1:
Why I wrote this book

Drinking sugar-loaded drinks has been "sanctified,"
and this sanctification has caused major problems
in the Pentecostal church. The belief is that alcoholic
beverages are bad because they intoxicate, but the
non-alcoholic sugary drinks are okay because they
don't intoxicate. While this is true, as far as the issue
of intoxication goes, the danger of sugary drinks is
the negative health impacts and the addictive nature
of sugar. The issue of drinking a lot of sugary drinks
is not only a Pentecostal problem. It is a problem that
is plaguing people from many different backgrounds.
There is a global obesity epidemic that is on the

rise with no end in sight. One of the main culprits is processed sugar.

I wrote this book to raise awareness and to initiate discussions about this troubling issue. It is a tough issue to tackle because the Bible is "silent" about it. Religious people of the Book, such as myself, like things that are clearly taught by scripture. This makes it easier for us to follow the instructions that have been given.

But when it comes to non-alcoholic, sugar-loaded drinks, it is the Wild West, and everything goes. The danger is that many people are comfortable drinking large quantities of sugary drinks because they are sweet and seem harmless. Many of the people drinking sugary drinks are unaware of the addictive nature of sugar and how it can ruin their health. Therefore, something must be done to raise awareness and help people to break free from the bondage of sugar.

The sugar corporations are enormous, and their marketing of such a harmful product is so sleek that many have fallen prey to it without knowing. The destruction that sugar is causing cannot be ignored, and now is the time to confront these problems.

There is little being said in pulpits across the world about the dangers of non-alcoholic, sugar-loaded drinks. But much is being said about the dangers of alcohol. Both are equally dangerous! I believe that non-alcoholic drinks are more dangerous because people do not drink with any moderation. Since these drinks are "safe," many unsuspecting people have fallen prey to the addictive nature of sugar, and it is ruining their lives.

Alcohol is being flagged for being dangerous to our health and it is time sugary drinks be flagged as well.

When you visit events that are organized by Bible-believing people, there is zero alcohol, and rightfully so. But what's so troubling is the abundance of sugar-loaded drinks that are served. Sugary drinks have become ubiquitous among Bible-believing brethren.

The whole idea that processed sugar is "safe" and can be consumed without question needs to be challenged. Part of the reason this book was written is to shed much-needed light on this problem.

The addictive nature of alcohol is a well-known fact, and people are encouraged to be aware of it, yet sugar (which is also addictive) is given a free pass. I want to inform those drinking sugar that it is addictive. They may think they are just drinking the sugar because it is sweet, but the truth is that they have developed a dependency on the substance. And it is not going to be easy for them to break free because sugar already has a firm grip on them.

In most countries, a legal age to drink alcohol has been established, and it is enforced. But for sugar, children as young as a day old are introduced to it. Why is it so? Because we have been sold a lie that sugar is safe and healthy. You hear arguments like "every carbohydrate eventually breaks down to sugar." Yes, that's true, but what sugar are we talking about? There is a big difference between the monosaccharides (fructose, galactose, and glucose) and disaccharides (lactose, maltose, and sucrose).

Therefore, it is essential to understand that all sugars are not the same. When you eat fruit, while it has sugar, it also has fiber that has multiple health benefits. This is much different from adding processed sugar to a cup of tea or drinking a can of soda that is loaded with sugar.

Industry-sponsored research may give the impression that sugar is not nearly as bad as it truly is; we, as consumers, must understand and watch what we put in our bodies. You must not drink the sugar: period! Do not put junk in your body.

In the past, sugar was expensive and not nearly as abundant and cheap as it is today. But the availability of cheap sugar can be correlated to the rise in obesity globally. In short, the introduction of the western diet is usually followed by an increase in obesity. This is a trend that has been observed all over the world. And it is obvious that there is a surplus of processed sugars and sugar-loaded drinks in western diets.

As a society, we are overindulging in sugar, and it is not good for our health. While we are waiting for government legislation to regulate this dangerous product, individuals must take things in their own hands by controlling the amount of sugar they allow in their diet.

My heart cries out to my brothers and sisters who have been conditioned to drink sugar without questioning its health benefits. This book is a wake-up call for you to realize that sugar is bad for you, and you should stay away from it. Nobody cares about your health and wellbeing more than you. Therefore, you should rise and take charge of your health, for it is the most critical asset that you have.

I hope this book will provide enough information for you to make the necessary changes to place you on the path to excellent health. I have not drunk soda for over a decade, and I feel much better than I did ten years ago. And since I cut sugar, I have noticed that putting off weight and keeping it off has not been a struggle.

I do not have an issue with soft drink companies, any more than with breweries and tobacco manufacturers. Picking a fight with any of these companies would be pointless; instead, I can make a change with the power of my money. I can choose what type of companies and products I spend my money on.

You, as a consumer, have the same power with your money and should use it accordingly. You shouldn't worry about these companies shutting down and their employees becoming jobless. They will evolve and give the consumer what they want, which is exactly what they have been doing for years.

Would you knowingly eat poison? No? Then why would you drink sugary drinks when they are not good for you? Just as you don't drink alcohol because it is not healthy, you must stay away from sugary drinks as well. This will be one of the most important and impactful decisions you ever make. I wrote this book to encourage you to eliminate processed sugar and sugar-loaded drinks from your life.

Lastly, my heart cries out because so many have been misled by well-intentioned preachers and teachers who have steered the precious people of God towards drinking dangerous drinks, under the pretext that they are non-alcoholic, therefore, healthy. This assumption is wrong and must be corrected. That is the central message in this book, and I hope that you understand it and act on what you learn. You must take action by drinking water and avoiding drinks that have added sugars.

Chapter 2
True confession

You need to understand where I am coming from so you can appreciate why I am writing this book. So, I am going to walk you through my journey regarding drinking.

I was raised in a Pentecostal family; we attended church regularly and followed the Bible closely. So, from a young age, I was taught that drinking alcohol is bad for you. I will be forever grateful for those teachings because they have given me a solid foundation and have kept me away from alcohol.

My father was an educator and an elder in the Full Gospel Mission, the largest Pentecostal denomination in Cameroon. He drank before coming to faith, but after he became born again, he gave up alcohol and no longer allowed himself or his family to drink.

In Cameroon, where I was born and raised, alcohol is readily available, and it is not uncommon for minors to drink. While there are laws that restrict minors from drinking, they are loosely enforced. For example, parents would send their children to go and buy alcoholic beverages when guests came over. When these children would go buy these drinks, nobody would ask them for any identification or proof of age. And in some cases, the children would be less than seven years old.

Some parents even allowed their children to drink a bit. By doing so, they initiated these children into drinking at an early age. When you are raised in a country where the biggest industry is the brewery, you must be cautious about the devastating impact of alcohol.

As a result of this abundance of alcohol and easy access, there is a lot of alcohol abuse in the country, and many people are addicted. Unfortunately, there are no alcohol rehabilitation programs in the country.

My father did not want any of us drinking alcohol and made sure that everybody around us knew it. He would always tell people that he didn't want the brains of his children to be fried. This taught me that there was a correlation between drinking and not doing well in school. I wanted to do well in school, so I took my father's prohibition seriously and stayed away from alcohol.

I will forever be grateful for what my father did because he was a great example of how to live an alcohol-free life. The only drawback was that while we were living alcohol-free, we were still encouraged to drink soda pop. Sugar-loaded bottled drinks were given to us during special events; for example, when a visitor came to visit, we would have the opportunity to drink soda pop. But this was not something that we practiced daily.

The ultimate test.

When I completed secondary school, I was about sixteen years old and was beginning to make my own decisions. Around that time, my father, my brother, and I all went to visit a family friend. As was the custom, they offered us some drinks, and we were given the option between alcoholic and non-alcoholic beverages.

My father took a non-alcoholic beverage, while my brother and I took beer; to my surprise, he didn't object to us drinking it. I don't know why he allowed us to drink the beer, and I haven't asked him.

After a few sips of the beer, I was done; it tasted bitter, and it made me wonder why people bothered drinking something so gross. From that day forward, I decided not to drink beer, but to stick to my sweet drinks. And in my mind, I couldn't go wrong drinking sugary drinks because they were sweet but non-alcoholic, so they didn't pose a threat.

Making our own sugary drinks.

Welcome to Brasseries de back Mbon! In Cameroon, the largest brewery company is Brasseries du Cameroun, or Breweries of Cameroon. The church my friends and I attended was located behind Mbon. So, we jokingly named our operation Brasseries de back Mbon.

When I went to high school, my friends and I had to make drinks for different functions that the church held, such as weddings and large gatherings. The making of the drinks was motivated by the belief that sugar is not bad and that you could drink as much as your belly can hold.

The operation was simple and straightforward. We would blend fruits such as pineapples, guava, papaya, and oranges, then dilute the concentrate with water and add sugar to make it sweeter. The drinks would then be chilled and served.

During all of this, it never occurred to me that there was anything wrong with sugar. I did not connect the dots between sugar and health because I was never taught that processed sugar was bad for us.

The only thing we cared about was that sugar is sweet, so it was therefore, it was suitable to consume. It never crossed our minds that there could be anything wrong with drinking soda and other sugary drinks.

Occasional drinking.

It is necessary to mention that drinking soda and other sugary drinks was a treat and not something that we did daily. Occasionally, when we had a guest visiting, we might have the opportunity to drink soda, but it was usually just a glass. One of the few times that I was given a full bottle of soda to drink was December 25th. The celebration of Christmas meant that we had an opportunity to drink a lot of sugary drinks. But during the rest of the year, we drank water. At least this was the practice in my home.

Many kids that I grew up with did not drink soda daily, especially those of us that were raised in the rural area. In the cities, the situation was a little different because people tended to be more affluent and had easier access to these sugary drinks.

When I moved to the city to attend college, I drank a little soda because I no longer had to wait for Christmas. Yet it still was not something I did daily.

Drink-all-you-can bonanza.

After I received my bachelor's degree, I moved to the United States of America for graduate school, and I was shocked by what I found. I could not believe my eyes when I had my first hamburger at Burger King and was told that I could drink all the soda I wanted at the soda fountain. Wow! From scarcity to abundance. I had never seen a soda fountain before and was mesmerized by the possibility of drinking as much and as many different varieties of soda as possible.

It was not long until I found out that I could drink soda every day, and just skip water if I chose to. The soda was cheap and readily available. And in my mind, soda was still non-alcoholic, and there was no fear that it was bad for me.

When I went to the supermarket, I could not believe what I saw. There were so many different juice brands on display, and all were loaded with sugar and cheap.

Take a drink like chocolate malt; I remember how little chocolate malt we bought and drank when I was

What's in Your Glass?

a kid because malt was a little more expensive and harder to find. But here in the US, it was cheap and abundant.

Limiting the amount of soda.

Before I moved to the US, one of my uncles told me to be careful about how I ate because the food could get me into trouble. He told me this because he noticed an excessive weight gain in other immigrants that had lived in the country longer. I took his advice to heart and was conscious of how much soda I drank. Something just seemed wrong with drinking soda every day. So, I started rationing how much soda I drank; I tried to only drink soda every other day.

Limiting the amount of soda and other sugary drinks was a challenge because those types of drinks were everywhere I went. I came to America during the summer, and the temperature was hotter than anything I had ever experienced before. Under such weather conditions, nothing tasted more refreshing than a cold soda. And I began to understand why people had such strong cravings to drink more. I soon realized that it was, in part, the addictive nature of sugar that caused people to develop cravings. Secondly, the salt in the soda would make me feel thirsty, so I wanted to drink more.

I was setting myself up for serious problems because even with all my rationing, I drank more soda in the first few months of being in the US than I had ever drunk in my life.

16

Eliminate soda completely.

As time went on, my knowledge about the dangers of soda grew, yet I struggled with giving it up. Let's face it, sugar is sweet, and there is nothing more refreshing than a cold Coke in the middle of a hot summer day.

After a few years in the country, my wife quit soda cold-turkey; I tried to mirror her efforts, but would still drink a soda here and there, especially when we went out of the house.

Then I stopped completely. It will soon be a decade that I have not drunk a soda. When we stopped drinking soda, we replaced it with juices, but that too has become obsolete in our diet because most juices these days are diluted juice loaded with sugar, carbon dioxide, water, and preservatives.

This explains why freshly squeezed orange juice tastes differently from the orange juice on the shelves. But this freshly squeezed orange juice is also more expensive.

Cost is what drives a lot of people to drink artificially flavored sugar water. They want to drink large quantities, so they buy the cheap stuff because they can get more for their money. In reality, it is better to drink a small glass of natural juice that contains fruit than a big liter of colored water.

In addition to, I do not add sugar to my tea or any other hot beverages. I am not a regular coffee-drinker, and on the few occasions I drink coffee, no sugar is added.

You can see that this war against sugar goes beyond sugar-loaded drinks. My wife even posts #sugarsucks and #sugarisakiller. Can you stop reading and share this hashtag on your different social media platforms? Thank you for doing that.

Don't think that I am crazy for suggesting that you should eliminate sugar from your diet. I did not do it in a single day. It is a process, and I hope that you will carefully consider the information presented in this book and make an informed decision.

We are not supposed to be controlled by anything. If you have cravings for stuff like milkshakes, ice cream, soda pop or other sugary items and find you can't control those impulses, it is time for you to make a change. The choice is yours, and nobody else can make it for you.

Just because other people drink sugary drinks does not mean that you have to drink them as well. You can never go wrong with drinking water.

The benefit of giving up soda.

Giving up soda and many other sugary drinks has healed me of body itches that I used to get when I drank them. It is difficult to explain how uncomfortable I would feel after taking a shower. Immediately after I stepped out of the shower, my body would start to itch, and it would make me feel like never taking another bath! This was something that I just had to put up with. I didn't stop drinking soda because I wanted the itching to stop, but when I did, I was pleasantly surprised to find that the itchiness went away, and it hasn't returned since.

The other big thing is my waistline; it has decreased, and after almost twenty years in the US, my waistline has barely changed. In fact, I took off ten pounds about nine years ago and have kept it off.

In addition to having my weight under control, my blood sugar is excellent, and my energy level is high. All the frequent urination in the night and breaking out in sweats have ceased, and I feel great.

Another benefit is not having any more cavities - for both my children and me. I remember how my first son developed cavities when we had just moved to the US. Since I was a student living off a student stipend, we qualified for a special supplemental nutrition program for women, infants, and children (WIC). Before our son came to the country, his teeth were beautiful, but that changed when we started giving him the WIC-recommended juices. These were concentrates which required us to add water to turn them into juice. The amount of sugar in these juices was high. Over time our son developed cavities, but ever since we moved away from sugary drinks, none of our children have developed any new ones.

Now that we know better, we have tried to steer our children away from sugary drinks and candy. They even refuse candy when offered to them because they understand the drawbacks of consuming processed sugar.

Do not buy soda at all.

Many people wonder how I have managed to go almost ten years without drinking sugar. In the beginning, it wasn't easy because I kept having the cravings, but over the years, the cravings have died down, and I am completely free.

My family and I have been able to stay soda-free because we simply do not buy sodas when we go out to shop. This helps keep our house a soda-free zone. Therefore, when the temptation to drink soda hits, it is not a readily available option for us. I have found the strategy of not buying soda and bringing it into the house to be very effective. There are those who buy the soda, bring it home, then say they will not drink it. This is like trying to pick up fire with your hands and expecting to not get burned.

Many people become vulnerable when they are tired, hungry, or thirsty, and they will succumb to their temptation and drink soda. Then, after failing a few times, they will convince themselves that it is too hard and that they are a failure. And they will give up altogether. The truth is that they are not failures. They have what it takes to be sugar-free if they would only remove the temptation from their house.

There have been times that I had strong cravings for something sweet to drink. When those cravings hit, I go to the refrigerator, open it, and look for something sweet. And even though I know there is nothing in there, I check the pantry. The outcome is predictable! There is nothing to drink, so I end up drinking water, perhaps squeezing some lemon into it to change the taste.

It is a daily struggle, especially in the US, where sugar is cheap and ubiquitous. One must make a conscious effort to avoid consuming too much sugar. This is a daily battle that can be won if you are intentional, disciplined, and determined in what you are doing.

Do not get overwhelmed thinking about sugary drinks. By the time you are done reading this book, you will know what to do. Keep your eye on the bigger picture. Many people dismiss conversations about health, claiming, "We are going to die anyway, so why does it matter?" And they are right! We are not focusing on preventing death, because death is inevitable, but the quality of life. But the quality of life is what we are talking about. Do not let the years that you have to live be filled with sickness and health challenges because of an unhealthy lifestyle.

Prevention is better than cure! One way to prevent the myriad of illnesses that sugar can induce in our bodies is by not eating the sugar in the first place. This may not be what you were expecting to hear, but I am writing this out of love and concern for your well-being. There is much more to life than drinking sugar and becoming sick. Just as you do not drink alcohol, it is important for you not to drink sugar as well. Alcohol is dangerous because it harms the body, and in similar ways, sugar has a lot of negative impacts on the body as well.

One last thing:

You need to understand that all the information presented in this book is for you to learn about changes that can affect you positively. This is not an attempt to impose my personal convictions on you. At the end of the day, it is your life, and you make the decisions. I hope that this book will equip you to make informed choices. While I have shared my convictions, it is left to you to make your own choice.

Therefore, choose wisely; whatever choice you make, you and you alone will live with the consequences.

To drink or not to drink is a decision that must be made after careful consideration. It does not matter if the drink is alcoholic or not; you should not let your guard down when it comes to drinking anything except water. Some have argued that if it is not an alcoholic drink, it can be consumed without question. They may not state this implicitly, but their attitude towards sugary drinks speaks volumes.

When there is a function where sugary beverages are served, people are normally allowed to drink without restrictions. At least when it comes to alcoholic beverages, people are given limits so that they cannot drink and drive. This helps to prevent some people from drinking excessively. But when it comes to sugary drinks, there appears to be no restriction. After all, Jesus Christ turned water into non-alcoholic wine. Is this true? Is the wine that Jesus turned water into the same as the soda pop that we drink today?

In the next chapter, we will look at why the wine Jesus made at the wedding in Cana is nothing close to the sugary drinks we drink today. Follow me to Cana and let us take a close look at what transpired there.

Chapter 3
Jesus Christ turned water into wine

"That's the problem with drinking, I thought, as I poured myself a drink. If something bad happens you drink in an attempt to forget; if something good happens you drink in order to celebrate; and if nothing happens you drink to make something happen."

- Charles Bukowski

Jesus had been invited to a wedding in Cana, and there, he performed his first miracle. This first miracle was not raising the dead, healing the sick, or cleansing the lepers; Jesus simply turned water into an excellent wine. Can you imagine that?

The people hosting the wedding ran into a severe problem: they ran out of wine, and there was nothing they could do about it. So, Mary, the mother of Jesus, stepped in. It is interesting that before now, there is no mention of Mary interceding and asking Jesus to do anything for anybody. I do not know why she did not before, but finally, she did, and her request was an interesting one. She wanted her son to provide wine for the wedding party.

Take a minute and think about why Jesus would use his divine powers to make wine for a wedding. One would reason that the people had some wine, and now that it was finished, they should just forget about it. Why bother Jesus with something so basic and mundane as wine? Are there lessons He wanted to teach here or did He just make the wine for the sake of making it?

I think, at times, in our effort to spiritualize things, we read into scripture and see things that are not there and do not belong. The wedding in Cana was not a church wedding; it was a wedding that brought two families together because their children were getting married. It was a celebration in a house, not a church building, and it was not being officiated by a pastor or clergy person.

I was raised celebrating marriage in three separate and distinct occasions. The first celebration is called traditional marriage. This is when the groom goes to the family of the bride, and the bride is officially handed to him. After the bride is officially handed over, they go to court, where the marriage is conducted. This is a civil ceremony that involves signing the marriage certificate. Then the last ceremony is the church wedding. Here the pastors or ministers officiate the marriage. These three occasions of celebration are almost mandatory in the setting I was raised.

When I was a child, I thought the marriage in Cana was equivalent to a church wedding because Jesus was present. But that is not true; Jesus was invited to that wedding, and He was not even an officiating minister. There is no mention that He was an essential dignitary because He was not sitting at the high table. So, due to the absence of clergy or pastors and the setting of the wedding, we learn that it was a traditional wedding.

There is an essential detail of this miracle that must be mentioned, and this has to do with the quantity of wine that Jesus made. Biblical scholars estimate the amount of wine to be between 120 to 180 gallons, or 454 to 681 liters. After Jesus had turned water into wine, he asked the servants to draw the wine and take it to the master of ceremony - who was astonished at how excellent it was. This is a lot of wine, good wine at that, and it speaks to the generosity of Christ. He was not just interested in making wine, but He ensured that it was more than enough.

But why did Jesus make the wine after He just told His mother that His time had not yet come? What was it about this request and this wedding that moved Jesus to perform His first miracle here? Who starts his ministry by making wine for people to drink? One would expect a big, spectacular miracle like that was what the devil suggested Jesus should do.

> *"When the tempter came to Him, he said, 'If You are the Son of God, command that these stones become bread.' But He answered and said, 'It is written, Man shall not live by bread alone, but by every word that proceeds from the mouth of God.'*
>
> *Then the devil took Him up into the holy city, and set Him on the pinnacle of the temple; he said to Him, 'If You are the Son of God, throw*

Yourself down. For it is written, "He shall give His angels charge over you, and in their hands, they shall bear you up, lest you dash your foot against a stone."'

Jesus said to him, 'It is written again, "You shall not tempt the Lord your God."'"- (Matthew 4:3-7, NKJV)

Jesus refused to turn stones into bread, even though He was hungry after fasting for forty days. But when there was no wine at the wedding, He turned the water into wine. Why? The two circumstances are different but have to do with meeting physical needs.

When the devil could not get Jesus Christ to prove who He was, by turning stones into bread, he tried asking Jesus to do something spectacular. This was tempting because the devil even quoted the scriptures that had promised Jesus's protection. This was a great opportunity for Jesus to make a spectacular entry at the start of His ministry.

Imagine how people in Jerusalem would have responded to Jesus flying. Do you not think that this would have been a strong statement that Jesus was indeed the Messiah? It would have made it easier for people to believe in Him. If it were today, Jesus would go viral for jumping from the top of a skyscraper without any parachute and flying. All the major news networks, freelancers, and private citizens would capture every single moment and broadcast it.

Jesus refused to do spectacular miracles that would have brought Him great publicity. Instead, He accepted the opportunity to turn water into wine at an ordinary, obscure wedding that was not a "spiritual" activity.

Jesus cares about normal things.

A lot has been written about this passage because it deals with wine. My Pentecostal background insists that anything involving alcohol must be avoided completely. People who have this belief have difficulties understanding this miracle. Before we talk about whether the wine was alcoholic or not, it is important to come down from our spiritual high horse and just admit that Jesus cared about these people having a good time. While there may be thousand-and-one religious reasons and symbolism hidden in this first miracle, I am not going to try to decipher them because that is not the purpose of this book.

What is essential is that ordinary people had a typical need. That was to drink wine, and Jesus cared enough to provide for them, so much that He performed a miracle to gladden the hearts of these people on such a momentous occasion.

Jesus cared about normal things because He wanted to meet the needs of those around Him; He wasn't looking for attention.

Does Jesus care about us drinking sugar-loaded drinks?

I have gone through this long explanation because we need to understand that Jesus cares about us. What we drink matters because when He made the wine, it was good quality wine. If Jesus was at a wedding today, would He turn water into colored water loaded with sugar, carbon dioxide, artificial colors, and flavors?

The wine Jesus made was not soda, nor anything close to what we are being encouraged to drink under the disguise of "non-alcoholic wine." It is wrong to encourage people to drink *sugar water* (as my four-year-old son calls it). Although it is non-alcoholic, it's dangerous to the body. There are too many illnesses that are directly tied to the consumption of processed sugars.

Sanctioning the consumption of drinks with fructose corn syrup is misguided and must be called out for what it is. These modern-day drinks that pass as non-alcoholic beverages are nothing close to the wine that Jesus made for the people to drink at the wedding.

Was the wine Jesus made alcoholic or non-alcoholic wine?

There is no indication of the type of wine Jesus made, but a lot has been written about this wine. Some say the wine was sweet because the master of the ceremony said the wine was excellent. Others believe that the wine was alcoholic wine with the capacity to intoxicate those who drank it. The question is, would Jesus knowingly make an intoxicating drink and give it to people? This is not something Jesus Christ would do; He would not knowingly make more drinks for people to get drunk.

We are going to go with the assumption that the wine Jesus made was new, meaning it was wine that had not yet been fermented. In other words, it was freshly pressed grape juice. If this is the case, then Jesus made a drink that was not loaded with processed sugars, artificial flavors, and carbon dioxide.

The difference between freshly-pressed grape juice is like day and night when compared to what passes these days for non-alcoholic drinks. Most of these drinks are loaded with processed sugars in quantities that are not healthy for the human body. We are going to see that many modern-day illnesses can be traced to excessive artificial sugar consumption.

Although these non-alcoholic sugary drinks cannot make somebody drunk, they have the potential of causing more health damage than many are willing to accept.

A serious assumption with undesirable consequences.

Before we look at what the Bible has to say about wine, I am going to assume that soda and other artificial sugar-loaded drinks are "non-alcoholic wines." I say "I am assuming" because the impression I got growing up was that drinking these sugar-loaded drinks was a good substitute for alcoholic beverages.

This assumption must be made because it will permit us to see how the Bible treats the use of wine. In other words, I am trying to bring these drinks under the canopy of the *fruit of the vine*. Make this leap with me and let us see if prohibiting the drinking of these sugary drinks is Biblical.

When I say "prohibiting," I am referring to the treatment of fruit of the vine in the Bible, as we are about to see. This is being brought up because some will argue that the Bible is completely silent about sugary drinks and only talks about wine, therefore, we shouldn't say anything about these drinks.

But the issue I have is the fact that there are preachers who teach that instead of drinking wine, sugary drinks are an excellent substitute. In their minds, they have already chosen to equate sugary drinks to "fruit of the vine." This is an unfortunate situation that needs to be addressed.

We, the people of God, cannot in good faith continue to encourage each other to drink "poison" in the name of non-alcoholic beverages. The sugar addiction is getting out of control, and the devastating consequences of drinking these drinks is evident around us.

Forgive me for belaboring the point. When you visit a function organized by Pentecostals that firmly stand against the consumption of alcohol, it is awash with all sorts of sugar-loaded drinks. The sad thing is that many people think these drinks are safe for them to drink. But the truth is these drinks are dangerous and should not be served in the first place. When we get into the details of the amount of sugar in a can of coke and the damage that sugar does to the body, you will understand why it is time for the people of God to stop substituting these dangerous drinks for wine.

Sadly, these drinks are socially acceptable and "cool" to drink. We need to change this because these drinks pose their own dangers, just as alcoholic beverages do. The biggest drawback is that when you drink an alcoholic beverage and get drunk, you can tell immediately, but with these sugary drinks, they will slowly destroy you.

I keep on asking myself, how did we get here? Just because a drink is sweet in the mouth does not mean that it is good for the body. It seems the marketing manufacturers of these dangerous drinks have outsmarted us, or those who substitute these drinks for wine have misled us.

Either way, now is the moment of truth. I hope that just as preachers preach against alcohol, they will have the courage to preach against drinking sugar water. Who in their right mind drinks sugar water? It is high time somebody speaks up against these dangerous drinks.

If you think this is a joke, you should try giving up your sugary drinks and see what the withdrawal symptoms are going to be like. Right now, you may believe that you are in control and can stop drinking sugar anytime you want. The sad news is that it is going to be an uphill battle because the cravings are going to be stronger than you ever imagined. You will have to go through a detoxification process to get rid of the sugar in your system.

Let's see what the Bible has to say about drinking and how people have conducted themselves over the years.

Total prohibition of wine and anything to do with the vine.

There are instances in the Bible where (for a season) somebody who took the Nazirite vow was prohibited from drinking wine or eating anything that comes from the vine. Here are the exact instructions God gave Moses concerning this vow:

> *"Then the Lord spoke to Moses, saying, 'Speak to the children of Israel and say to them: When either a man or woman consecrates an offering to take the vow of a Nazirite, to separate himself to the Lord, he shall separate himself from wine and similar drink; he shall drink neither vinegar made from wine nor vinegar made from similar drink; neither shall he drink any grape juice, nor eat fresh grapes or raisins. All the days of his separation he shall eat nothing that is produced by the grapevine, from seed to skin.'"* (Numbers 6:1-4, NKJV)

Take note that the Nazirite was prohibited from eating fresh grapes and raisins during their time of separation to the Lord. This approach eliminated any chance of getting drunk.

Meet John the Baptist; he was told by God not to drink wine or any strong drink before he was born. This is what God instructed him to do:

> "But the angel said to him, 'Do not be afraid, Zacharias, for your prayer is heard; and your wife Elizabeth will bear you a son, and you shall call his name John. And you will have joy and gladness, and many will rejoice at his birth. For he will be great in the sight of the Lord, and shall drink neither wine nor strong drink. He will also be filled with the Holy Spirit, even from his mother's womb." (Luke 1:13-15, NKJV)

The injunction on John the Baptist not to drink was like that of Samson:

> "Now there was a certain man from Zorah, of the family Danites, whose name was Manoah; and his wife was barren and had no children. One day the Angel of the Lord appeared to the woman and said to her, 'Indeed now, you are barren and have borne no children, but you shall conceive and bear a son. Now, therefore, please be careful not to drink wine or similar drink, and not to eat anything unclean. For behold, you shall conceive and bear a son. And no razor shall come upon his head, for the child shall be a Nazirite to God from the womb; and he shall begin to deliver Israel out

of the hand of the Philistines.'" (Judges 13:2-5, NKJV)

There are some similarities between the circumstances surrounding the birth of John the Baptist and that of Samson. The parents of both John and Samson had struggled over the years to have a baby. In short, their mothers were barren, and the possibility of having a baby was zero.

When both parents were unexpectant, an angel of the Lord appeared to them with the good news that they were going to have sons.

Both parents were also instructed to ensure that their sons did not drink any wine or strong drink because God had a special assignment for them. This was going to be a lifetime commitment. God fulfilled his promise and used these two men to do amazing things.

Some took it upon themselves not to drink at all.

This is a fascinating account of an entire family, the Rechabites, who took it upon themselves not to drink, even after the prophet of God gave them wine. It is written:

> *"The word which came to Jeremiah from the Lord in the days of Jehoiakim the son of Josiah, king of Judah, saying, 'Go to the house of the Rechabites, speak to them, and bring them into the house of the Lord, into one of*

*the chambers, and give them wine to drink.'
Then I took Jaazaniah the son of Jeremiah, the
son of Habazziniah, his brothers and all his
sons, and the whole house of the Rechabites,
and I brought them into the house of the Lord,
into the chamber of the sons of Hanan the son
of Igdaliah, a man of God, which was by the
chamber of the princes, above the chamber of
Maaseiah the son of Shallum, the keeper of the
door. Then I set before the sons of the house
of the Rechabites bowls full of wine, and cups;
and I said to them, 'Drink wine.' But they said,
'We will drink no wine, for Jonadab the son of
Rechab, our father, commanded us, saying,
"You shall drink no wine, you nor your sons,
forever. You shall not build a house, sow seed,
plant a vineyard, nor have any of these; but
all your days you shall dwell in tents, that you
may live many days in the land where you are
sojourners." Thus we have obeyed the voice of
Jonadab the son of Rechab, our father, in all
that he charged us, to drink no wine all our
days, we, our wives, our sons, or our daughters,
nor to build ourselves houses to dwell in; nor
do we have vineyard, field, or seed. But we
have dwelt in tents and have obeyed and
done according to all that Jonadab our father
commanded us.'"* (Jeremiah 35:1-10, NKJV)
(Note: emphases in bold are my own)

Interestingly, these people were brought to the house
of the Lord and offered wine, and they refused to

drink. We can argue all day whether this wine was non-alcoholic or alcoholic. But the simple fact is that this family was not going to have any wine no matter the type, period! They gave up wine because their father had instructed them not to drink. It did not matter if the wine was sweet or bitter or aged or unaged. Their father told them you shall not to drink any wine, and they took it to heart and obeyed him; they even rejected a direct word from God.

I know what some are saying right now about such an "extreme" position. What harm would a glass of wine do to these people? What about them being a good guest and honoring the prophet by drinking a little wine? Wasn't it bad that this family was disobeying God by refusing to drink?

You are going to be surprised by how God himself responded to this "extreme" stance of the Rechabites. Here is what the Lord told them through Jeremiah the prophet:

> "And Jeremiah said to the house of the Rechabites, 'Thus says the Lord of hosts, the God of Israel: "Because you have obeyed the commandment of Jonadab your father, and kept all his precepts and done according to all that he commanded you, therefore thus says the Lord of hosts, the God of Israel: 'Jonadab the son of Rechab shall not lack a man to stand before Me forever.'"'" (Jeremiah 35:18-19, NKJV)

God commended them for being people of conviction because they had obeyed the command of their father.

It is important to understand the backstory of why God asked Jeremiah to ask the Rechabites to drink wine. This next passage is the heart of the matter, and the message God was conveying to His people:

> *"Then came the word of the Lord to Jeremiah, saying, 'Thus says the Lord of hosts, the God of Israel: "Go and tell the men of Judah and the inhabitants of Jerusalem, 'Will you not receive instruction to obey My words?' says the Lord. 'The words of Jonadab the son of Rechab, which he commanded his sons, not to drink wine, are performed; for to this day, they drink none and obey their father's commandment. But although I have spoken to you, rising early and speaking, you did not obey Me. I have also sent to you all My servants the prophets, rising up early and sending them, saying, "Turn now everyone from his evil way, amend your doings, and do not go after other gods to serve them; then you will dwell in the land which I have given you and your fathers." But you have not inclined your ear, nor obeyed Me. Surely the sons of Jonadab the son of Rechab have performed the commandment of their father, which he commanded them, but this people has not obeyed Me.'"'* (Jeremiah 35:12-16, NKJV)

The inhabitants of Jerusalem had refused to obey the word of God and the messages He was sending through his prophets. In contrast, the Rechabites were faithfully obeying the commands of their earthly father by refusing to drink wine.

This is a situation where people took it upon themselves not to drink wine, not because they were commanded by God, but by another human. Yet, it gained an eternal promise and blessing from God.

These people didn't say they were abstaining from wine because they wanted to live longer or avoid getting drunk. The reason for not drinking was because their father told them not to. Some would say that this must have been a very restrictive father who did not care about his children having any fun, but I can personally say my dad was prohibitive. And because of his rules, I have been saved from the struggles associated with alcohol.

We have to keep our focus on the bigger picture of why we are here on Earth and the mission that God has for us. Anything that will interfere with this mission must be put aside, including unhealthy beverages.

God gave us bodies to help those around us and as a place for the Holy Spirit to dwell. Therefore, we need to take good care of our bodies, because without a healthy functional body, we are physically useless.

Sugar is dangerous and has devastating consequences, yet, it is socially acceptable and has even been sanctified in some circles. Unfortunately, sugar is just as devastating in the long run as many other substances that people put in their bodies.

You don't need to look far to see people that have allowed alcohol, drugs, and other substances such as sugar to waste their bodies. We already have all the sugar that we need from the other foods we eat.

The issue with processed and refined sugars is that they are added to our diet without the accompanying roughage that comes with eating whole fruits.

Those who drink alcohol have developed a taste for it. When I was growing up, I heard those who drank alcohol mocking those of us who drank only soda. They said that we were not manly enough to drink something strong. But those of us who drank sweet drinks pitied those who were addicted to alcohol, and we felt justified because sugary drinks could not make you drunk.

I now understand that drunkenness is not the only issue that we should be concerned about. We should be concerned about things like obesity, heart disease, diabetes, acne, cancer, depression, accelerated aging, energy drain, fatty livers, kidney disease, cavities, accelerated cognitive decline, and gout.[1]

Sugar is just unfermented alcohol, and because it is unfermented it cannot make us drunk, but because of the connection between sugar and alcohol, we must scrutinize sugar to the same degree.

I'm not saying that cutting out sugar and alcohol is going to make us live forever. The focus is on quality of life and our health because the body is a vehicle that we use to carry out the mission God has given us. Therefore, it is essential to take care of our bodies both inside and out.

Most of us take care of our bodies on the outside, by bathing frequently, making sure that we groom

---

[1] https://www.healthline.com/nutrition/too-much-sugar

ourselves, and dressing appropriately. But when it comes to taking care of the inside, many treat their body like some sort of junkyard where anything can be dumped without giving a second thought to what it would do.

Whenever you are eating or drinking, you must understand that the food is going into your body and will become a part of you. This is why allowing your taste buds to be the sole arbitrator of what you eat and drink will land you in a lot of trouble.

So far, we have seen that the Bible is silent on sugar-loaded drinks, but as a society, we have started using them the way we used sweet or non-alcoholic wine. In other words, wine includes soda, fruit juices, and all other non-alcoholic drinks that have added sugar.

It is impossible to talk about drinking without looking at wine and what the Bible teaches about it. We have already seen that there are two positions, to drink or not to drink wine or anything related to the fruit of the vine.

What the Bible teaches about wine and strong drink.

God made the vine, and the first time we hear of anybody planting the grapes and making wine, drunkenness is also mentioned. Noah, after the flood, planted the first vineyard and ended up drunk from drinking wine. Because of his drunkenness, he exposed his nakedness to one of his sons. When Noah became sober, he cursed his son.

I am going to digress a little here to say that: the cursed son did not transfer that curse to people from Africa, which has been taught by some and is still being propagated. Some people used this curse as an excuse to justify slavery, segregation, and discrimination against people of African descent.

You can see how devastating the consequences of Noah's drunkenness have been over millennia. Can you believe that some of the inhumane treatment of African slaves who were people of darker skin pigmentation was justified by the curse of Noah? As preposterous as that may sound, it is a fact. I was shocked when, not too long ago, I heard an old tape of a preacher from the South in the 1950s claiming that people with darker skin were descendants of Shem and were cursed. Because they were cursed, they were inferior and couldn't be treated as equals. This is a doctrine from the pit of hell, and it should be denounced.

The saddest part is that there are African preachers who still believe this lie and are propagating it. Noah got drunk, cursed his son, and that is all.

No wonder the Bible takes drunkenness seriously and prohibits it. God is not against us having fun or a good time, but He loves us so much that He does not want us to destroy ourselves. There is no other passage of scripture that describes the devastating effects of alcohol better than the following:

"Who has woe?

Who has sorrow?

Who has contentions?

Who has complaints?

Who has wounds without cause?

Who has redness of eyes?

Those who linger long at the wine,

Those who go in search of mixed wine.

Do not look on the wine when it is red,

When it sparkles in the cup,

When it swirls around smoothly.

At the last it bites like a serpent,

And stings like a viper.

Your eyes will see strange things,

And your heart will utter perverse things.

Yes, you will be like one who lies down in the midst of the sea,

Or like one who lies at the top of the mast, saying:

'They have struck me, but I was not hurt;

They have beaten me, but I did not feel it.

When shall I awake, that I may seek another drink?'"

(Proverbs 23:29-35, NKJV)

I have never been drunk, so I cannot describe what happens when you are under the influence, but I have heard too many sad stories to mention. Alcohol will render you useless and make you see and do strange things.

I heard about a mother who came from Africa to visit her children in the United States. They took her to a function at a friend's house, and at that function, beer and other alcoholic beverages were in abundance, and the mother got drunk. Then she did the unthinkable; she pulled down her dress and started urinating in the middle of the living room. The embarrassment and shame that she caused may never go away.

Some pass out and pee, vomit, or poop on themselves. Alcohol indeed stings like a viper when you linger under its influence. When breweries are advertising alcohol, they never show people who have been rendered hopeless and reduced to rags and shame. All you see are happy faces, but behind those smiling faces are individuals who are in bondage.

But some people argue that it is their life, and drinking doesn't affect anyone but themselves; they say that they are only destroying their body, and it is their life. This type of selfish argument is useless. If you are human and live in a society with others, you cannot claim that your actions do not impact other people. When you get drunk and allow alcohol to destroy you, it is depriving other people of the services that you were created to perform. Can you imagine what could happen if everyone were drunk in your community and passed out? Who would come and put out the flames of a fire? Who would clean the streets? Who would teach your children in school? How would you get treatment if you became sick? Would it be possible to drive on the roads if everyone were drunk? We were created for relationships and have to ensure that we do our part because if we don't, then we won't have a strong, healthy, and functional society.

The other thing that makes drunkenness dangerous is the impact it has on other people, especially when people get drunk and get behind the wheel. According to the United States Department of Transportation, about 30 people die each day as a result of drunk driving. In 2017, one person died every 48 minutes; over the course of that year, about 100,000 people died, and the total cost of damages caused by crashes in 2010 was about $44 billion.[2]

At times when you read about statistics like this, they do not fully affect you until you meet people who have been impacted directly. For example, last week, one of my students missed coming to a lab because she had to attend the funeral of two friends. These were two sisters of her boyfriend who were killed on the same day by a drunk driver. The drunk driver ran a red light at an intersection, rammed into their car, and killed them both on the spot. Their father was driving and survived the crash but had severe injuries; also in the car was their stepmother, who sustained injuries as well. Can you imagine how profoundly this family was impacted by alcohol? Even though they themselves were sober, they weren't safe.

I will never forget one Cameroonian lady who was also killed by a drunk driver; she had just finished school, got a job, and was preparing to bring her husband over. She was coming back from work when

---

[2] https://www.nhtsa.gov/risky-driving/drunk-driving

the vehicle broke down on the highway. She sat in the car, trying to make some calls and get help. As she was waiting for help, a drunk driver ran into her car and killed her and the baby in her womb.

I can go on and on with these types of stories because they occur more often than they should. When you look at the careers, marriages, and families that have been ruined by alcohol, you can understand that not drinking may be the wisest thing to do.

King Solomon continued his advice on drinking and says some profound things about alcohol here:

> *"It is not for kings, O Lemuel,*
>
> *It is not for kings to drink wine,*
>
> *Nor for princes intoxicating drink;*
>
> *Lest they drink and forget the law,*
>
> *And pervert the justice of all the afflicted.*
>
> *Give strong drink to him who is perishing,*
>
> *And wine to those who are bitter of heart.*
>
> *Let him drink and forget his poverty,*
>
> *And remember his misery no more."*
>
> (Proverbs 31:4-7, NKJV)

Drinking wine can make people forget things, including the law. In other words, your ability to judge appropriately is compromised. This includes judging distances, especially when driving.

Drunkenness is gluttony and is strongly prohibited in the Bible. There are too many scriptures that command us not to get drunk. Some people have the personal discipline to drink just a single glass of wine. But this is not the case for all who have fallen into the trap of alcoholism. Alcohol is a chemical that can cause people to become addicted and dependent on it. Therefore, the best way to stay clear of becoming addicted is not to drink in the first place. The benefits of drinking, if any, pale in comparison to those of not drinking.

We are living in trying times, and Paul the Apostle wrote the following words of admonition on how we should conduct ourselves:

> *"See then that you walk circumspectly, not as fools but as wise, redeeming the time, because the days are evil. Therefore, do not be unwise, but understand what the will of the Lord is. And do not be drunk with wine, in which is dissipation; but be filled with the Spirit."* (Ephesians 5:15-18, NKJV)

Fools linger around strong drink and end up drinking more than they can handle. When you are under the influence of alcohol, you will not be able to think straight, and you will take risks. Why would you want to be under the influence of a substance that can mess up your life? We are promised the gift of the Holy Spirit. Jesus Christ said that He was leaving, so the Holy Spirit (who is our comforter) would come to be with us always.

People who are pro-alcohol-consumption do not have good reasons. When I was a kid, I heard that WHISKY means, Watch How I Slowly Kill You. You get the point! Alcohol has destroyed too many lives, careers, and marriages so there is no reason to mess with it.

Drunkenness is a sin.

The Bible is very clear about drunkenness being a sin and the consequences of living in sin. The following portion of scripture teaches that drunkenness is a sin:

> *"Now the works of the flesh are evident, which are: adultery, fornication, uncleanness, lewdness, idolatry, sorcery, hatred, contentions, jealousies, outbursts of wrath, selfish ambitions, dissensions, heresies, envy, murders, drunkenness, revelries, and the like; of which I tell you beforehand, just as I also told you in time past, that those who practice such things will not inherit the kingdom of God."* (Galatians 5:19-21, NKJV)

Many other things here are listed as sin, and each of them is just as bad as alcohol addiction. When you take each of the sins named in this verse, you will realize that they are all works of the flesh (we use one of our five senses to indulge in them).

The risk for those who get drunk is incredibly high. If you do not amend your ways, you are going to forfeit the kingdom of God. This is a pretty serious warning and should not be taken lightly by anybody who loves God and wants to spend eternity with Him.

If you are reading this and know that alcohol has a strong hold over your life and you are struggling to break free, you should not give up, because Jesus Christ died for your sins and will give you a fresh start. You can reach out for help at eternalkingdom101@gmail.com. I want you to know that support is available and that you are not alone. You might have had many failures and defeats, and the enemy may be telling you that you should give up and stop trying, but I am telling you that victory is closer than you think. If you can admit that you have a problem with alcohol and stop trying to rationalize and justify it, you will get solutions. It is going to require denying yourself, but you have what it takes to do it.

But Jesus drank wine...

Earlier, we learned that at conception, John the Baptist was set aside for an assignment. His parents were instructed to ensure that John did not drink any wine. Scripture tells us that John lived in the desert and ate honey and wild locusts. He did not drink wine, for Jesus Christ himself said the following about him:

> *"For John the Baptist came neither eating bread nor drinking wine, and you say, 'He has a demon.' The Son of Man has come eating and drinking, and you say, 'Look, a glutton and a winebibber, a friend of tax collectors and sinners!' But wisdom is justified by all her children."* (Luke 7:33-35, NKJV)

Jesus Christ said, *"Those who are well, do not need a doctor, but the sick are those who look for a doctor."* He came to heal the sick and to look for the lost. While the Pharisees, scribes, and teachers of the law segregated themselves from those they considered to be lost, Jesus did the opposite by eating with these people (to eat with people back then was a sign of accepting them and identifying with them).

Therefore, the Pharisees and the teachers of the law took issue with Jesus Christ for eating and drinking with tax collectors and sinners. The accusation that Jesus Christ was a glutton and drunkard was slander from these teachers of the law who were looking for a way to discredit Jesus Christ. These men felt that the Ministry of Jesus was threatening their position and livelihood, and they were not going to stand by while He took everything from them.

This was not the only time that these men had falsely accused Jesus Christ and tried to discredit him. Take, for example, the woman whom Jesus had cast demons out of; she brought an expensive perfume and poured it on the feet of Jesus then used her hair to wipe His feet. The Pharisees and teachers of the law were shocked that Jesus was allowing this prostitute and chief sinner to touch Him. They thought that if Jesus were a true prophet, He would have known who this woman was and would have prevented her from touching Him.

When the Pharisees, scribes, and the high priest could not contain Jesus Christ any longer, they conspired to kill Him. They did this by framing Christ and used false charges to crucify Him.

Saying that Jesus was a drunkard and glutton is not at all accurate. There has never been any sinless person except Jesus Christ. Therefore, He was not a drunkard and glutton. This means that those who justify drinking and getting drunk under the pretext that Jesus drank as well, should reconsider their position on this matter. Jesus did not drink to get drunk. If you are drinking and getting drunk, then you are not following the example of Jesus Christ. You are doing your own thing, and it is time to repent and change your ways.

"Take a little wine for your stomach's sake."

You can twist the Bible into saying whatever you want. Here is one of the most misquoted Bible verses by those who attempt to justify drinking alcohol:

> *"No longer drink only water but use a little wine for your stomach's sake and your frequent infirmities."* (1 Timothy 5:23, NKJV)

Paul, the Apostle was giving Timothy instructions to use wine to help with some stomach issues that he was having. But some people use this verse as an excuse to get drunk. What they fail to understand is that they are not like Timothy - who had a stomach ailment. The instructions say that he should take *"a little wine."* But today, people do not take a little; they drink large quantities.

Some believers get drunk, and when questioned, they insist that they follow Timothy's example. But

Timothy did not get drunk, so they are not following the instructions that were given to Timothy.

We are called to live in freedom and should not be under the bondage of anything, including the substances we drink and the food that we eat. If you are arguing that you must drink wine because Jesus drank and that Paul instructed Timothy to drink a little wine for his stomach's sake, make sure that you are free of drunkenness. Some people misuse this verse, and the little bit of wine always becomes larger quantities. Those addicted to alcohol will tell you that it would have been better if they had never tasted the first drop.

Just like any other addiction, the best way to prevent becoming addicted is by not starting in the first place.

I commend the Pentecostals' stance on alcoholic beverages.

The dangers of drinking alcohol far outweigh the benefits. It is not worth the risk to start drinking in the first place. In the Old Testament, those who took the vow to be set apart for God were prohibited from drinking alcohol or anything from the grapevine. If God sets people aside and part of the requirement is for them to stay away from alcohol, then we should seriously consider the validity of staying sober all the time.

The emphasis by the Pentecostals on zero alcohol is good, and they should be commended. The probability that I will ever be an alcoholic is zero;

I did not develop the habit of drinking because of my Pentecostal upbringing and the strictness of my father, who ensured that we did not drink alcohol when I was young. I will be forever grateful for this heritage.

While celebrating such a legacy, it is necessary to take a closer look at the heritage of sugar. Nothing I write here is meant to put anybody down. I firmly believe that a lack of awareness is the culprit here. The blame lies squarely with the producers and marketers of these products. They have given full disclosure to the general public about the dangers that drinking sugar poses, but the information that is usually displayed on the drinks is not explicit enough. You should not be required to be a mathematician to figure out how much sugar is in a can of soda. At times, the salt that is added in the soda is reported as sodium. Many people are clueless about the relationship between sodium and salt. The chemical formula of salt is NaCl. Yet when you take a close look at the soda, you will read that salt was added in the drink. The added salt makes you thirsty and makes you want to drink more. When salt and sugar are combined, the taste buds cannot resist it. Sugar on its own is addictive, and it becomes more dangerous when it is combined with salt. If you have been wondering why it is difficult for you to stop drinking soda, this is probably one of the reasons

As we are going to see soon, the issue goes beyond the sugar; the problem is also the salt that is added. My intention is not to wage war against the manufactures of these sugar-loaded drinks. These companies have deeper pockets than me and are well-positioned to fight anybody who dares to challenge them.

My goal is to bring awareness about the poisonous nature of drinking excessive sugar, and how dangerous it is to the health of those who consume it daily. The first step to freedom is awareness. The manufacturers of these drinks do not force anybody to buy their drinks, but they market them aggressively and do not give the proper disclaimers to the public. While we wait for appropriate legislation that will address some of these issues, we will continue with the effort to educate the public about the dangers of drinking sugary drinks, or sweet drinks in general.

With proper education, more and more people will choose life over death and health over sickness. Nobody wants to die prematurely because of what they drink. But many being destroyed by sugar have not been told about the dangers associated with their diet. I was in this category while growing up and it is not too long ago that I came to my senses.

In the next chapter, we are going to take a close look at sugar and see why this white substance is a poison and causing a worldwide obesity epidemic. While sugar tastes sweet in the mouth, it has a "bitter" effect on those who drink or eat it in large quantities. After you read the next chapter, you will be ready to make up your mind about what to do with sweet drinks.

Chapter 4
The inconvenient truth about sugar

Is it true that sugar is eight times more addictive than cocaine? Is sugar even addictive? If sugar is that addictive, why is it legal and readily available and accessible? But there is sugar in fruits, how can sugar be bad? All carbohydrates are broken down into sugar that the body burns for energy. How can this source of energy be bad? The science on the harmful effects of sugar is not conclusive. We do not know enough to come to any clear conclusions. If sugar was that bad, there would be a war against sugar, just like there is a war against drugs.

Another industry had similar questions and as-sumptions, but the day came when the truth prevailed. For many years, the tobacco industry lied to the general public about the dangers of smoking, especially the relationship between smoking and cancer. Industries backed studies, muddied the waters, and confused the general public about the dangers of smoking. Meanwhile, independent researchers were consistently pointing out the dangers of smoking, nicotine addiction, and different kinds of cancers tobacco could cause. But big money and big industrial interests trumped the health of the people. As a result, thousands - if not millions - died from using tobacco. Now warnings such as these are placed on cigarette packs:

"SURGEON GENERAL'S WARNING: Smoking Causes Lung Cancer, Heart Disease, Emphysema, and May Complicate Pregnancy."

"SURGEON GENERAL'S WARNING: Quitting Smoking Now Greatly Reduces Serious Risks to Your Health."

"SURGEON GENERAL'S WARNING: Smoking by Pregnant Women May Result in Fetal Injury, Premature Birth, and Low Birth Weight."

SURGEON GENERAL'S WARNING: Cigarette Smoke Contains Carbon Monoxide.[3]

While these warnings can't prevent everyone from smoking, it has raised the level of awareness so that fewer people are smoking compared to when it was popularly believed that smoking was harmless.

---

[3] https://www.cdc.gov/tobacco/data_statistics/ sgr/2000/highlights/labels/index.htm

A day is coming when the truth about sugar will be exposed. The present amount of sugar we consume cannot continue. The consequences are enormous. While the debate is heating up and people are taking sides, I think the consumer has more power than they think. You will have to learn how to use the power of your purse to influence the direction our society takes against sugar. With our influence, we can make the demand weak so that the supply will falter. It is unwise to place your health in the hands of other people. There is nothing more important than doing everything within your power to figure out what you should eat and drink. Whatever we eat is going to affect how our body operates. Therefore, you should care about what you eat and drink. Sugar is one of those substances that should be monitored closely.

Before I say anything about sugar and what other studies are saying, nobody puts it better than Gary Taubes. In "The Case Against Sugar," Gary Taubes writes the following:

> *"Imagine a drug that can intoxicate us, can infuse us with energy, and can do so when taken by mouth. It doesn't have to be injected, smoked, or snorted for us to experience its sublime and soothing effects. Imagine that it mixes well with virtually every food and particularly liquids, and that when given to infants it provokes a feeling of pleasure so profound and intense that its pursuit becomes a driving force throughout their lives. Overconsumption of this drug may have long-*

term side effects, but there are none in the short term—no staggering or dizziness, no slurring of speech, no passing out or drifting away, no heart palpitations or respiratory distress. When it is given to children, its effects may be only more extreme variations on the apparently natural emotional roller coaster of childhood, from the initial intoxication to the tantrums and whining of what may or may not be withdrawal a few hours later. More than anything, our imaginary drug makes children happy, at least for the period during which they're consuming it. It calms their distress, eases their pain, focuses their attention, and then leaves them excited and full of joy until the dose wears off. The only downside is that children will come to expect another dose, perhaps to demand it, on a regular basis. How long would it be before parents took to using our imaginary drug to calm their children when necessary, to alleviate pain, to prevent outbursts of unhappiness, or to distract attention? And once the drug became identified with pleasure, how long before it was used to celebrate birthdays, a soccer game, good grades at school? How long before it became a way to communicate love and celebrate happiness? How long before no gathering of family and friends was complete without it, before major holidays and celebrations were defined in part by the use of this drug to assure pleasure? How *long would it be before the underprivileged of the world would happily spend what little money they had on this drug rather than on nutritious meals for their families?"*

While the debate about the merits and demerits of consuming sugar is raging on, it would be wise to focus on cutting back as much processed sugars as users can from their diet. It is a fact that the increase in the consumption of sugar is linked to the advent of diabetes and many other diseases. So, while the smart thing to do is stay away from sugar as much as possible, it is best if you can eliminate it from your diet.

The inconvenient truth about sugar.

We are looking at sugar because it is the main component in all the soda and all the other sugary drinks that are consumed regularly. Sugar, as we have already said, seems innocent and tastes sweet. Is it bad even if it tastes so good? Before you accuse me of being biased about sugar, I will suggest that you consult the following sources that deal with the negative impact of the sugar in our diet on our health. Before you discard what is being said here, take some time and look up these sources:

- Sugar can cause gallstones[4]

---

[4] Harvard Women's Health Watch 2011. What to do about gallstones. [Online]. [Accessed 01 June 2011]. Available from: https://www.health.harvard.edu/womens-health/what-to-do-about-gallstones

- Sugar contributes to adrenal fatigue[5]
- Sugar can suppress your immune system[6]
- Sugar raises the level of neurotransmitters called serotonin[7]
- Sugar weakens eyesight[8]
- Sugar can cause hypoglycemia (low blood sugar levels)[9]
- Sugar can cause aging[10]

---

[5] Walsh, Bryan. The Adrenal Glands. [Online]. [Accessed 01 June 2019]. Available from: https://www.health.harvard.edu/womens-health/what-to-do-about-gallstones

[6] Reinagel, D.M., 2018. Does Sugar Really Suppress the Immune System? [Online]. [Accessed 01 June 2019]. Available from: https://www.scientificamerican.com/article/does-sugar-really-suppress-the-immune-system/?redirect=1

[7] Lustig, R.H., 2012. The Most Unhappy of Pleasures: This Is Your Brain on Sugar. [Online]. [Accessed 01 June 2019]. Available from: https://www.theatlantic.com/health/archive/2012/02/the-most-unhappy-of-pleasures-this-is-your-brain-on-sugar/253341/

[8] Hitti, M., 2017. High-Sugar Foods May Affect Eyesight. [Online]. [Accessed 01 June 2019]. Available from: https://www.webmd.com/eye-health/macular-degeneration/news/20070713/high-sugar-foods-may-affect-eyesight

[9] Mayo Clinic Staff 00. Hypoglycemia. [Online]. [Accessed 01 June 2019]. Available from: https://www.mayoclinic.org/diseases-conditions/hypoglycemia/symptoms-causes/syc-20373685

[10] Leith-Manos, R, 2013. Is sugar aging you?. [Online]. [Accessed 01 June 2019]. Available from: https://www.smh.com.au/lifestyle/beauty/is-sugar-ageing-you-20130513-2jib2.html

- Sugar can contribute to eczema[11]
- Sugar increases bad cholesterol and triglycerides[12]
- Sugar makes you eat more[13]
- Sugar can lead to leptin resistance which will result in weight gain and sleep trouble[14]
- Sugar stresses the liver[15]
- Sugar causes weight gain
- Sugar can cause pancreatic cancer
- Sugar can cause kidney disease
- Sugar can cause high blood pressure

---

[11] Katta, R., Desai, S.p., 2014. The Role of Dietary Intervention in Skin Disease. The Journal of Clinical and Aesthetic Dermatology, 7 (7), pp. 46–51.

[12] Heart and Vascular Institute, 2018. Cholesterol and Sugar: Is Something Sweet Turning Your Cholesterol Sour?. [Online]. [Accessed 01 June 2019]. Available from: https://share.upmc.com/2018/06/cholesterol-and-sugar/

[13] Kubala, J., 2019. Cholesterol and Sugar: Is Something Sweet Turning Your Cholesterol Sour?. [Online]. [Accessed 01 June 2019]. Available from: https://www.healthline.com/nutrition/does-sugar-make-you-fat

[14] Kondracki, N. L., 2012. The Link Between Sleep and Weight Gain — Research Shows Poor Sleep Quality Raises Obesity and Chronic Disease Risk. Enter Name of Periodical. [Online]. 14 (6), pp. 6. [Accessed 01 June 2019]. Available from: https://www.todaysdietitian.com/newarchives/060112p48.shtml

[15] University of California San Francisco, SugarScience 00. The Toxic Truth: Too much fructose can damage your liver, just like too much alcohol. [Online]. [Accessed 01 June 2019]. Available from: https://sugarscience.ucsf.edu/the-toxic-truth/#.XPMmd4hKjcs

- Sugar contributes to cognitive decline
- Sugar can cause gout
- Sugar can cause insulin resistance
- Sugar promotes wrinkling and aging skin
- Sugar makes your blood acidic
- Sugar can lead to osteoporosis
- Sugar rots your teeth
- Sugar raises your blood sugar level
- Sugar contributes to obesity
- Sugar is addictive
- Sugar can create the urge to binge
- Sugar provides "empty calories" with no nutritional value
- Sugar contributes to diabetes
- Sugar robs your body of minerals
- Sugar robs you of energy
- Sugar contributes to heart problems
- Sugar can cause cancer
- Sugar contributes to ulcers
- Sugar can cause inflammation
- Sugar can cause acne[16]
- Sugar causes insulin resistance
- Sugar causes depression
- Sugar causes anxiety
- Sugar causes heartburn

---

[16] Smith RN1, Mann NJ, Braue A, Mäkeläinen H, Varigos, GA., 2007. The effect of a high-protein, low glycemic-load diet versus a conventional, high glycemic-load diet on biochemical parameters associated with acne vulgaris: a randomized, investigator-masked, controlled trial. Enter Name of Periodical, 57 (2), pp. 247–256.

Which of the disease will you choose?

The list of possible diseases that are associated with sugar presented above are not the only ones, but this should be enough for you to understand the dangers associated with sugar.

The answer to the question "What disease will you choose?" is **none.** But talk is cheap! Everybody will say that they do not want to be obese, have heart disease or cancer, but their actions don't show it. What they eat and drink daily says that they want to have these diseases, you cannot keep drinking sugar yet expect not to be affected. The definition of insanity is doing the same thing over and over, expecting to have different results.

Many people will say that they value their health and will do everything in their power to live healthy lives. But they cannot give up their sugary drinks and other forms of sugar. There is a significant disconnection between what they claim to desire and their actions.

One of my students recounted a sad story about his father, who was diagnosed with type-2 diabetes. We were talking about healthy living, and he told us that his father chose to die rather than change. He said he was going to die anyway, and there was no point in doing anything about it. He decided he was going to enjoy the last few days he was having by eating whatever he wanted. So, rather than making a change, he just continued down the path of destruction, and finally got destroyed.

Just like him, some will read this book and choose to continue down the path of destruction. According to them, sugar is cheap, readily available, and sweet, so much so, they would rather indulge in it than live.

Please do not get me wrong. We are all going to die, and the purpose of staying away from sugary drinks is not to prevent death. It is about the quality of your life. If you are alive, you should be able to do the things that you desire to do. It is better to eat healthily than be unable to be active.

My prayers and hope for you are that you will not only say you will choose good health and life but also live it out. If you are one of those who talk but do not walk the talk, you can make a change right now. Don't expect this to be easy. Although it is tough, it does not mean that you cannot do it. If you have not been fasting regularly, you will have to learn how to fast. Please do not get scared because the word fasting has been mentioned. Fasting is an ancient practice, and even Jesus Christ fasted for forty days. Many other great fathers of the faith fasted. This will be tough, but you will have to do it if you strongly desire to break the yoke of sugar in your life.

Do your homework!

I deliberately include as many references as possible so that you can start the journey of discovery for yourself. What we are talking about is a matter of life and death. Therefore, you should invest the time, energy, and resources to investigate this issue for yourself. Do not take my words for it. Check the references included in here, then go beyond that. Do not say that your family has always lived like this, and there is no point changing. Are you happy with where you are right now? Do you like the quality of your health, fitness, and wellness? Are you satisfied with the doctor's report concerning your health? If you are pleased with where you are, and your health is in great shape, good for you! Feel free to disregard what I have to say. But if you are not who you want to be, I implore you to study so that you can make an informed decision. Do not continue reading this book without consulting the references included above.

While our goal is not to live here on Earth forever, the few years you have here must be productive ones. Your productivity will be hampered if you are living in poor health. The way you can prevent poor health is by eating and drinking in a way that builds your fitness instead of destroying it.

Do not say that you already know everything about sugar because if you knew you would not be consuming the amount of sugar you have been consuming. It is one thing to say that you know and an entirely different thing to act on your knowledge.

Show me what you claim that you know by what you do. Our actions speak louder than our words. You can pretend, lie, and hide, but what you do reflects what you know.

It is going to be difficult for you to turn around and drink large quantities of sugar after you have told people that sugar is not suitable for them. The more you educate other people, the easier it is going to be for you to overcome your sugar addiction.

Fasting from sugar.

If you think you are not addicted to sugar, you may be mistaken. Here is a challenge for you to see if you will have withdrawal symptoms when you try to stay away from sugar.

Do a one-week fast from sugar. This is going to be one week of zero sugar. Meaning, you will eat no cakes, not soda, no juices - *nothing that has processed sugar.* There is no cheating. You will be allowed to drink water only. No flavored water. Just plain water!

The push-back and withdrawal symptoms you are going to face will be a wakeup call for you. It is not going to be as easy as it sounds, and you may not even make it through one week without eating or drinking processed sugar because the cravings are going to be so strong, beyond what you ever imagined or thought possible.

But you are going to be amazed by the changes that will occur in your body during this one week. If you have eaten and drunk a lot of sugar throughout your life, this will be the only time that you are giving your body a break.

It will be essential to document the changes in your body by taking pictures each day. By the end of the seven days, take a close look at the pictures, paying close attention to changes in your skin.

You should weigh yourself before you start, then weigh yourself at the end of the seven days and see how many pounds you have lost. You will be amazed by many pounds you lose in just one week of not eating any sugar.

ACTION

Start a one-week fast from sugar now, before you continue reading the book.

Take the "100 days of clean eating and exercise challenge."

Now that you have finished the one week fast from sugar, it is time for you to take on a more significant challenge. If you benefited so much from one week of not eating or drinking sugar, imagine how much you benefit from 100 days of not eating or drinking sugar. In addition to not consuming sugar, you will be adding exercise to your life.

Again, what we are aiming at here is your quality of life. Nobody said that you would not be sick or unhealthy. Being occasionally ill is okay but being sick all the time and not being able to take care of yourself, your family, and your loved ones is not acceptable. Anything that interferes with the mission that God has given you should not be tolerated. Anything that is against the best that God has planned for you should not be tolerated by you. Healing is the children's bread.

Before we take a closer look at this 100-day challenge, I want you to consider a few things. The Word of God has so many promises about health, wealth, productivity, and general wellbeing. You must evaluate the current condition of your life with these promises in mind. I must mention this powerful Psalm of David, which beautifully paints a picture of what a righteous life is supposed to be:

"Blessed is the man

Who walks not in the counsel of the ungodly,

Nor stands in the path of sinners,

Nor sits in the seat of the scornful;

But his delight is in the law of the Lord,

And in His law he meditates day and night.

He shall be like a tree

Planted by the rivers of water,

That brings forth its fruit in its season,

Whose leaf also shall not wither;

And whatever he does shall prosper."

(Psalm 1:1-4, NKJV)

How can you prosper when you are in ill health? Is health not true wealth? The symbolism of a tree planted by rivers of water is a powerful one. It talks of abundant supply for nourishment and eventually of high productivity. A tree needs water to be healthy because trees that produce fruit must be healthy. That is why the psalmist is talking about the leaves of the tree not withering. If the leaves of a tree wither, there is no way that tree is going to produce any fruit. Without any leaves, the tree will die because the tree - through a process of photosynthesis - captures and stores the sun's energy through the leaves.

Water is so crucial in this process because it dissolves the nutrients in the soil that the tree needs and helps to transfer them from the soil through the roots of the plants. Water also helps to keep the tree cool. Trees need to be cool as well; if not, they will wither and die.

We know that without water, there is no life. Our bodies are made up of between sixty-five to seventy percent water, depending on our age. When you add abundant water plus the energy of the sun to a tree, it will be healthy and productive.

How healthy are you? How productive are you? We have already mentioned so many diseases that are directly and indirectly related to sugar consumption. Are you suffering from any of these diseases? If you are suffering from any of these diseases, are they hampering your productivity?

The psalm is crystal clear about the outcome of the lives of those who spend time in the Word of God and meditate upon it. If your life is not like this, then you need to do something about it. Here is your opportunity to take charge of your health and become productive.

One week of staying away from consuming sugar is not enough to deliver what you need. Our lives are governed by habits. The purpose of the "100 Days of Clean Eating and Exercise Challenge" is for you to form the habits that will deliver to you the good health that you need.

The author of the "100 Days of Clean Eating and Exercise Challenge" was diagnosed with high blood pressure, and her doctor told her that seventy percent of the patients on high blood pressure medication could get off their medication if they made some lifestyle changes, such as exercising regularly. So, she decided to start exercising, and within one month her blood pressure went down to normal, and she went off her medication. For over a decade now, she has made exercising regularly part of her life and is teaching other people how to live a holistic lifestyle.

Any sustainable change must start in the mind. That is why there are two books that you need to succeed in this proven system. The first book, which is geared towards behavioral modification, is called "100 Days to Freedom: A Holistic Approach to Nutrition, Health, Fitness, and Wellness," which is where you should begin. This will change your mind and help you position yourself to live a holistic lifestyle. According to the author, *"A holistic approach to nutrition, health, fitness, and wellness is the only way to achieve sustainable and lasting results. Fads that are in the market right now may bring quick results, but many people relapse and get back into their old ways. Many have given up altogether because they are tired and burnt out from the 'yo-yo' dance involved in some of these solutions. I'm offering you an alternative that has been tried and tested for almost a decade, and it draws its inspiration from ancient wisdom. The foundation is based on the truth that transcends all cultures and is thousands of years old."*[17]

ACTION

Order the book on "100 Days to Freedom: A Holistic Approach to Nutrition, Health, Fitness, and Wellness."

---

[17] Tayem, E.A. 2018. 100 Days to Freedom: A Holistic Approach to Nutrition, Health, Fitness, and Wellness. 1 ed. Richardson: IEM Press.

Talk is cheap! If you do not walk the talk, don't expect any results. Even if you are eagerly anticipating results without doing the work required, you will not get anything. You will be given a proven system that will change your life for the better. After you have transformed your mind, the next thing is for you to get the "100 Days of Clean Eating and Exercise Challenge," a companion workbook to "100 Days to Freedom: A Holistic Approach to Nutrition, Health, Fitness, and Wellness."

> Here is what the author says about this resource:
> *"This resource was born because it took me more than a decade of uncountable false starts and failures for me to finally figure out how to persistently and consistently eat right and exercise regularly. The results have been phenomenal, and this caused many people to reach out to me with questions. Most of the questions have centered around how I did it and what my main motivation is. It dawned on me that many people are failing not because they lack will power or they are not motivated enough, or they don't want it enough. What they lack are the following: a strong WHY, mental toughness, and a practical system of accountability that can guide and support them to form the habits that will make them unstoppable."*[18]

---

[18] Tayem, E.A. 2018. 100 - day clean eating and exercise

ACTION

Order the book called "100 Days of Clean Eating and Exercise Challenge," a companion workbook to "100 Days to Freedom: A Holistic Approach to Nutrition, Health, Fitness, and Wellness."

Walking the talk has never been so easy. Here is your opportunity to do something that will have a fundamental impact on your health in a way that you never imagined. Seize this opportunity and make the most of it. You are going to be glad you did. There is an online community of people who are taking this journey by doing a total makeover of their thought process and body, and you are invited to join this community at no charge. This group is called the "100 Days of Clean Eating and Exercise Challenge," https://www.facebook.com/groups/1980000172293684/

***ACTION ***

- Go to Facebook and join this support and accountability group and start documenting your journey: https://www.facebook.com/groups/1980000172293684/
- Join our mailing list by sending an email to: cleaneatingin100days@gmail.com
- If you have any questions also email us at: cleaneatingin100days@gmail.com

---

challenge a companion workbook to 100 Days to Freedom: A Holistic Approach to Nutrition, Health, Fitness, and Wellness. . 1 ed. Richardson: IEM Press.

Educate other people.

We learn a second time when we teach other people. You will become an ambassador for healthy living, especially a sugar-free life. It is not going to be easy, but if you want to succeed, you will have to think about other people. It is not always about us, but what we can do for others. All of us have received a lot from God, and much more is expected of us. You have been blessed tremendously through this book and have learned so much. Now is the time for you to give back by teaching other people and helping them to get their health under control.

Don't say that you are not yet ready or that you do not know enough. Do you remember the woman who met Jesus at the well? She had such a powerful, transformative encounter that she ran to the village and invited the entire village to come to meet the man who had done so much for her within such a short time.

Were you able to stay for one week without sugar? Is this something that you thought you would be able to do? Did you notice any changes? Then now is your opportunity to share how you have benefited with other people. The sharing will benefit you more than those you are helping, because it is always more blessed to give than to receive.

Here is your opportunity to give hope, encouragement, and good health to other people. Join the movement against sugar and help liberate other people that have been held captive by the destructive power of sugar. You can make a life-changing and profound difference in their lives by just sharing your own experience.

Knowledge alone is not enough.

If knowledge alone were the only thing needed for change, many people would be off sugar. Unfortunately, acquiring knowledge is just the first step. You must gain understanding. It is only after you apply this knowledge that you will get the desired results. Have you ever heard somebody say, "I know," yet their action is diametrically opposite to what they are saying that they know? Take, for example, you tell a loved one or friend about the dangers of smoking or driving under the influence, and they tell you that they know. But they keep smoking and driving anyway.

Is this some sort of a disconnect, or what? What is knowing? Can you identify and not do? The answer is that if you know, you must do it. If you say that you know but are not doing, it implies that you just have head knowledge. Unfortunately, head knowledge alone is not enough.

Here is one of the most powerful scriptures that talk about the connection between knowing and doing:

> *"Therefore, lay aside all filthiness and overflow of wickedness, and receive with meekness the implanted word, which is able to save your souls. But be doers of the word, and not hearers only, deceiving yourselves. For if anyone is a hearer of the word and not a doer, he is like a man observing his natural*

face in a mirror; for he observes himself, goes away, and immediately forgets what kind of man he was." (James 1:21-24, NKJV)

Does it make sense to walk to the mirror, look at your face, and refuse to take away the dirt on your face? The only explanation for such an action is that you are blind, or your mirror is not right. But everything else being equal, we expect any normal person to do something about their looks when they look into the mirror. This is common sense.

The same common sense applies to many other areas of our lives, including what we do with information that pertains to our health. You must act because if you do not, you are deceiving yourself. Before you started reading this book, you had one attitude towards sugar and sugary drinks. Now is the time to act! If you do not act, nothing is going to change.

The futility of just believing.

Many people believe many things that are not true. Just because you believe it does not mean that you are correct. Some believe that drinking sugary drinks will do them no harm. Some even claim that they have prayed, and God has sanctified the drink, and all will be well with them. Are they putting the Lord God to the test? Why will you knowingly drink poison? What point are you trying to prove? If you think that this is a demonstration of faith, I will suggest that it is misguided faith.

There is another category of believing that falls under things that are true. For example, you may believe that drinking and driving are dangerous, or that drinking sugar will kill you. Yet you do not stop drinking. Of what use is this belief? Let me submit that it is useless to you because your belief has not changed your action.

Let James the Apostle shade some more practical light on this issue of faith and action, and belief and action:

> "What does it profit, my brethren, if someone says he has faith but does not have works? Can faith save him? If a brother or sister is naked and destitute of daily food, and one of you says to them, 'Depart in peace, be warmed and filled,' but you do not give them the things which are needed for the body, what does it profit? Thus, also faith by itself, if it does not have works, is dead. But someone will say, 'You have faith, and I have works.' Show me your faith without your works, and I will show you my faith by my works. **You believe that there is one God. You do well. Even the demons believe—and tremble!** But do you not know, O foolish man, that faith without works is dead?"

(James 2:14-20, NKJV)

(Note: emphasis in bold are my own)

The relationship between faith and action cannot be more apparent than as presented here. Show me your faith by what you do and not what you say you believe. Even the demons believe in God, yet they rebelled against God.

Many people say that they believe the promises of God concerning good health, prosperity, and living disease-free. Of what use is this belief if you keep drinking sugar and other things that are not healthy for you? This is being foolish. Who has deceived you? Don't you know that drinking sugar will kill you? If you did not have that information, now you do. A lot has been written about the dangers of sugar. Therefore, you cannot claim to be ignorant. In other words, the mirror has been held directly in your face.

You must do something if you want results. There is nothing else for you but cutting out sugar from your diet. This is going to be difficult, but it is doable. Just do it, and you will be glad you did.

Staying away from processed sugar is not a suicide mission.

What is the way forward, now that you know sugar is not good for you? Is a life without artificial sugar possible? Is it even desirable to get on this sugar-free path?

The information that has been presented in this book concerning sugar is information that you could not quickly get by Googling the harmful effects of sugar. Here are a few questions that you have to ask yourself. Why is it that obesity, type-2 diabetes, and other diseases related to sugar are on the rise? Why is it that people have this information yet chose not to do anything about it? Are people consciously choosing death over life or poor health over good health?

This implies that staying away from sugar is an excellent thing to do. The increase in sugar consumption is linked to these diseases; you will be doing yourself a lot of good if you stay away from sugar. In short, you lose nothing if you stay away from sugar.

Instead, if you refuse to stay away from sugar and insist on consuming sugar, you will be doing yourself a disservice. Consider the following sobering statistics about the increase in sugar consumption across the globe.

The consumption of sugar worldwide is on the rise, and this has been accompanied by non-communicable diseases such as cancer, diabetes, and heart diseases. These diseases now kill more people than infectious diseases. According to the World Health Organization, about 41 million people die each year as a result of non-communicable diseases (NCDs); this accounts for about 71% of all deaths globally.[19]

Here is where these stats get even more distressing; according to the report, 15 million people between the ages of 30 to 69 years died prematurely from NCDs.

---

[19] World Health Organization 2018. Noncommunicable diseases. [Online]. [Accessed 01 June 2019]. Available from: https://www.who.int/news-room/fact-sheets/detail/noncommunicable-diseases

Will you knowingly choose to die prematurely? The answer again is obviously NO. But your actions may just be saying the opposite. If you insist on drinking and eating sugar the way you are doing, you are saying that you want to die prematurely. Why will you choose sugar over life? Whatever excuse you have for eating and drinking the way you are doing does not matter. What matters is that you do what is right for your body and your health.

This implies that you should stay away from sugar. You just have to do that. I am sorry to disappoint you. But life without artificial and highly processed sugar is possible. You will have to make some changes and should not be afraid to make them. The excellent health that you will step into is going to be worth every ounce of sugar that you say away from.

If you still doubt if sugar is that bad for you, let us take a closer look at what is in the soda and other sugary drinks that are being sold to us. In the next chapter, we will be looking at the composition of sugary beverages.

Chapter 5
The devil is in the details!

> "'I was amazed to learn,' he testified,
> 'that the beverage contained substantial
> amounts of phosphoric acid. . .. At the
> Naval Medical Research Institute, we
> put human teeth in a cola beverage and
> found they softened and started to dissolve
> within a short period... The acidity of cola
> beverages ... is about the same as vinegar.
> The sugar content masks the acidity, and
> children little realize they are drinking this
> strange mixture of phosphoric acid, sugar,
> caffeine, coloring, and flavoring matter."
>
> ---Dr. McCay

Do you know what is in the sugary drinks that you regularly consume and even give to your kids? Have you ever taken a soda can and studied its contents, or do you just drink it because it is something that you are used to, and everybody is doing? By the time you are done reading this chapter, you will be wary of lifting another sugary drink to your lips. Don't be deceived by the cute pictures on the labels of these drinks. The manufacturers don't care about your health. What they are after is your money. Don't trust their words; do your homework. The manufactures are getting away with products that are not in the best interest of the general public because of a public that is being misinformed. Most people are under the false impression that sugar is perfectly fine to consume. It is sweet; therefore, it cannot be harmful.

Most people who drink soda are doing it under the assumption that it is legal and safe. They reason that if there were anything terrible with sugary drinks, they would not be advertised and sold publicly as they are being sold right now. The reasoning is that other bad things have been declared illegal and have been banned. If people are found with these prohibited substances, they face the consequences.

In fact, there is a war against drugs, and the government in many different countries spends millions each year fighting against these illicit drugs. But there is not war against sugar.

What these people fail to understand is the fact that the absence of war against refined and processed sugar does not mean that sugar is good for human consumption in the long run.

The other thing people need to understand is that just because a product is sold on the shelves of a supermarket does not mean that this product is healthy for human consumption. Sugar is so ubiquitous in our time that it is almost impossible to avoid consuming it.

In this chapter, we are going to take a close look at the content of soda. We are focusing on soda, energy, and sports drinks because according to the Center for Disease Control (CDC) forty-five percent of the added sugar in your diet comes from the sugary drinks you consume.[20]

While knowledge alone is not enough, it is the beginning of change. You should know what is in the soda that you are regularly drinking. Your body is not a junkyard, and you should not be drinking stuff without thinking about it. If people knew precisely what soda is, they would never allow a drop of it to touch their lips. The solution is not diet alternatives. Just stick with water because you cannot go wrong with the best solution that your body was engineered for.

Nobody in their right mind buys a car that is supposed to run on gasoline and puts diesel in the car. To ensure that your vehicle operates at maximum capacity, you should follow the owner's manual. Although it feels fine to put any type of fuel in your car, it does not mean the vehicle will operate using just anything you put inside.

The content of soda and other sugary drinks.

Let's take a look at some of what you drink when you consume soda and other sugary drinks. You will realize that the "devil" is in the details; it is not possible to cover all the different sodas out there and

---

[20] Harvard Men's Health Watch, 2017. The sweet danger of sugar. [Online]. [Accessed 01 June 2019]. Available from: https://www.health.harvard.edu/heart-health/the-sweet-danger-of-sugar

every sugary drink in the market. I will not be naming any names because some of the companies may come for me. You are the consumer and should use your discretion. The essential ingredients in soda drinks will be similar and in different quantities. If any drink is not freshly squeezed fruits, you should beware of what you are buying.

Here is the typical composition of soda as culled from the website, ThoughtCo:

- Carbonated water
- Sugar (which can be sucrose or high-fructose corn syrup)
- Caffeine
- Phosphoric acid v. caramel (E150d)
- Natural flavorings (which include coca leaf extract). In the past this particular soda contained cocaine. [21]

---

[21] Helmenstine 2019. Ingredients in Coke and Their Function What's Really in Coca Cola?. [Online]. [Accessed 01 October 2019]. Available from: https://www.thoughtco.com/the-ingredients-and-their-function-in-coke-explained-3976096#targetText=Coke%20contains%20a%20fairly%20short,Caffeine

Nutrition Facts

1 Serving Per Container

Serving Size	**1 Can**

Amount Per Serving

Calories 140

	% Daily Value
Total Fat 0g	**0%**
Sodium 45mg	**2%**
Total Carbohydrate 39g	**14%**
Total Sugars 39g	
Includes 39g Added Sugars	**78%**
Cholesterol 0mg	**0%**
Protein 0g	
Vitamin D	**0%**
Calcium	**0%**
Iron	**0%**
Potassium	**0%**

"Not a significant source of fat, *trans* fat, cholesterol, dietary fiber, vitamin D, calcium, iron, and potassium. Caffeine Content: 34 mg/12 fl oz"

The website also lists the following information regarding GMO:

"This product includes ingredients sourced from genetically engineered (GE) crops, commonly known as GMOs."[22]

Nutrition Facts

1 serving per container

Serving Size 12 fl oz (360 mL)

Amount Per Serving

Calories 150

% Daily Value*

Total Fat 0g **0%**

Sodium 30mg **1%**

Total Carbohydrate 41g **15%**

Total Sugars 41g

Includes 41g Added Sugars **83%**

Protein 0g

Not a significant source of other nutrients.

*%DV = % Daily Value

CARBONATED WATER, HIGH FRUCTOSE CORN SYRUP, CARAMEL COLOR, SUGAR, PHOSPHORIC ACID, CAFFEINE, CITRIC ACID, NATURAL FLAVOR

Last updated on September 26, 2019

Culled from the PEPSICO Website[23]

---

[22] The Coca-Cola Co. Products facts. The sweet danger of sugar. [Online]. [Accessed 01 October 2019]. Available from: https://www.coca-colaproductfacts.com/en/products/coca-cola/original/12-oz/

[23] PEPSICO THE FACTS ABOUT YOUR FAVORITE BEVERAGES. [Online]. [Accessed 01 October 2019]. http://

What is the point?

Here is the point we are trying to make here. You should not be drinking these sugar drinks because one can of soda is more than seventy-five percent sugar. This is about 39 grams, which is equal to 9.75 teaspoons of sugar.[24] What you need to know is that that American Heart Association recommends that all your daily sugar intake from foods and drinks with added sugars such as soft drinks, candy, cakes, cookies, pies, sweetened yogurt, sweetened milk, cinnamon toast, waffles, desserts, etc. should be no more than six teaspoons for women and nine teaspoons for men.[25] The amount of sugar from just one can of soda already exceeds the daily allowable amount of added sugar an adult should consume. No wonder many people are running into a lot of health problems. When you add sugar from all other sources, you will realize that most people consume far more sugar than they should.

---

www.pepsicobeveragefacts.com/Home/Product?formula=35005*26*01-01&form=RTD&size=12

[24] Boyers, L., Corleone, J. How Many Teaspoons of Sugar Are There in a Can of Coke? [Online]. [Accessed 01 October 2019]. Available from: https://www.livestrong.com/article/283136-how-many-teaspoons-of-sugar-are-there-in-a-can-of-coke/

[25] AHA Added Sugars. [Online]. [Accessed 01 October 2019]. Available from: https://www heart.org/en/healthy-living/healthy-eating/eat-smart/sugar/added-sugars

Let's do the math. If you drink just one can of soda per day for thirty days, you would have consumed 39g*30 = 1,170 grams of sugar; in other words, 9.75 teaspoons*30 = 292.5 teaspoons of sugar. In terms of calories, we are looking at 156 calories*30 = 4,680 calories. Can you imagine that each month, you are adding 4,600 calories just from drinking a can of soda? What if you drink more than one can and eat a lot of other foods that have added sugar? Your situation will become much more dire.

Let's stay with the one can of soda a day and see how this translates to weight gain. According to the Jackson Siegelbaum Gastroenterology website, "it takes an extra 3500 calories to gain one pound of body weight."[26]This implies that consuming just a bottle of soda per day will lead to at least one pound of weight gain per month just from the soda. If you are consuming excess calories from added sugars in other products, you can do the math. You might have been wondering why your weight is going up. If you gain just a pound a month, you are looking at over ten pounds in a year. But weight gain is just one of the many things you need to worry about when you consume processed sugar. We have already seen that sugar causes many different illnesses and will negatively impact your quality of life and shorten your life span.

---

[26] Jackson Siegelbaum Gastroenterology. Increasing Calories. [Online]. [Accessed 01 October 2019]. Available from: https://www.gicare.com/gi-health-resources/increasing-calories/

When you read a news headline like this one—"Sugary drinks linked to 31 percent higher risk of early death, study finds"—what runs through your mind? This is a recent study conducted by Harvard University and published in the journal "Circulation". The study "found people who drink two or more sugar-sweetened beverages a day have a 31 percent higher risk of early death from cardiovascular disease. Each additional soda, sports drink, or sugary beverage increased the risk by 10 percent".[27]

You have only one body – don't put junk into it!

I am not going to beat a dead horse. By now, you understand the dangers of consuming processed sugar. But I do not know what you have decided to do with this information. It is not talking a lot about it that is going to make you change.

But I want you to consider one last thing. You only have one body, and what you do to it will determine your quality of life. Your body is the temple of the Holy Spirit, and you should treat it with care and respect.

The only person who will stop putting junk in your body is you, and you alone. What are you waiting for? Stop waiting for your appetite to lead the way. You are

---

[27] Welch, A. Sugary drinks linked to 31 percent higher risk of early death, study finds. [Online]. [Accessed 01 October 2019]. Available from: https://www.cbsnews.com/news/sugary-drinks-linked-to-higher-risk-of-early-death-study-finds/

the person in charge, and it is your responsibility to lead the way. Nobody cares about your health more than you. Therefore, stop waiting for government regulations to force sugar to be taken off the shelves in the supermarkets. This may never happen, but you can take away the sugar from your pantry.

Don't wait for others to lead the way for you. It is your life, and you should not be basing your decisions on what other people are doing. If sugar is bad, it is bad even if other people are consuming it.

Sugar is so ubiquitous these days that you need to be self-disciplined not to overeat it. In the middle of writing this portion, I went out for Night Day out in my street. There were a lot of sugary drinks, cookies, brownies, and other unhealthy snacks. One of my neighbors bought brownies, and I ate a little piece. Brownies had never tasted so sweet, maybe because I have not had any for such a long time. The temptation to eat another piece came up, and I gently but forcefully reminded myself that the little piece I had eaten was enough.

I do not remember the last time I ate a brownie before this, but I ran five miles this morning. This is something that I do five times a week averaging about thirty or more miles each week.

Unfortunately, many people eat all the wrong things but never exercise or even go out for a walk. Why are you destroying your own body? If you do not take care of your body, when it becomes too unfit for your soul to live in, your soul will leave. You *will* die!

Chapter 6
It is not a sin not to drink sugary drinks

> "'I have the right to do anything,' you say—
> but not everything is beneficial. 'I have the
> right to do anything'—but not everything
> is constructive".
>
> (1 Corinthians 10:23, NIV)

There is nothing sinful about drinking sugary drinks. But what is the point of writing an entire book to talk about sugary drinks? The issue is the negative consequences of drinking these drinks and how harmful they can be to those who consume them frequently. In chapters 4 and 5, you were presented with a lot of information on the detrimental effects of sugar and how dangerous sugary drinks are. Now is an opportunity for you to weigh the evidence and make an informed decision about what to do. The assumption is that you are a believer in the Lord Jesus Christ and look to the Bible as a source of inspiration and guidance. While the Bible does not explicitly talk about sugar and sugary drinks, it speaks about many other things that are related to how we conduct ourselves.

We are going to let the Paul the Apostle help us navigate through this challenging issue. This is not the first time that something has come up that is not black and white. Paul was dealing with the issue of eating meat offered to idols, and he said the following:

> ***"'I have the right to do anything,' you say—but not everything is beneficial. 'I have the right to do anything'"—but not everything is constructive.*** *No one should seek their own good, but the good of others. Eat anything sold in the meat market without raising questions of conscience, for, 'The earth is the Lord's, and everything in it.' If an unbeliever invites you to a meal and you want to go, eat whatever is put before you without raising questions of conscience. But if someone says to you, 'This has been offered in sacrifice,' then do not eat it, both for the sake of the one who told you and for the sake of conscience. I am referring to the other person's conscience, not yours. For why is my freedom being judged by another's conscience? If I take part in the meal with thankfulness, why am I denounced because of something I thank God for?* **So, whether you eat or drink or whatever you do, do it all for the glory of God.** *Do not cause anyone to stumble, whether Jews, Greeks, or the church of God— even as I try to please everyone in every way. For I am not seeking my own good but the good of many, so that they may be*

saved." (1 Corinthians 10:23-33, NIV) (Note:
emphases in bold are my own)

The issue is not whether sugary drinks are bad or not. We should be asking about how beneficial and constructive drinking sugar water is. While we have every right to drink whatever we want, we may opt not to because it is not beneficial and constructive.

I spent a considerable amount of time in chapter 3 discussing the first miracle of Jesus Christ that involved turning water into wine. The sole purpose was to look at drinking in general. It does not matter what we drink. The sole purpose of drinking is to give us pleasure, and, at times, to socialize with other people. Another reason is that of having comfort, especially during moments of tragedy and discomfort.

This implies that those who drink alcoholic beverages choose this as their drink of choice, and those who do not drink alcohol will choose sweet beverages. But the question we should be focusing on is the following: Is drinking beneficial and constructive? This does not matter if you are drinking alcohol or non-alcoholic beverages.

It has already been established that you can do whatever you want to do, but what is the outcome of your actions? In other words, if sweet drinks are as dangerous to the body as we have already pointed out, will you drink them because you think you can? Or will you prioritize your health and stay away from them? Would you rather drink, and deal with obesity, heart disease, type-2 diabetes, acne, cancer, depression, accelerated aging, energy drain, a fatty liver, kidney disease, cavities, accelerated cognitive decline, and gout?

I think the choice is obvious, but as we have already established, sugar is addictive, and many addicts live in denial. Many people who are addicted to sugar are living in denial as well. They do not want to admit that they have a problem because they have convinced themselves that something this sweet cannot be bad. Then how have you been able to explain your increasing waistline, low energy, cavities, type-2 diabetes, and many other ailments that you are presently struggling with?

Have you resorted to the blame game and victim mentality? It is not uncommon to hear people say, "This is the way I was born" or "All of our family are like this." Some go as far as to suggest that their genes are to be blamed for their present weight issue. If you have all or some of these complaints, you are correct. But you are not at the mercy of your family history and your environment, even the genetic predisposition to put on weight.

The issue is not that you lack self-will or may not be working out enough. If you keep drinking and eating the wrong things, you are not going to be able to burn them off. There are many different studies that have been carried out on animals in the wild, and time and again, it has been established that these animals have their weight under control. There seems to be a good balance between what they eat and how much they use.

But when animals in captivity are studied, we begin to see weight gain issues because these animals are not eating the right kinds of food. Therefore, the issue is with what you eat and drink. In this case, we are referring to sugary drinks, especially the fructose that is found in these drinks. The best thing to do is to avoid drinking these drinks. They may be sweet and look colorful and appetizing, but it does not mean that they are good for your health. The fact that many other people are drinking does not mean that you should drink. Even when the advertisers say that these drinks are good for you, you must do your homework. Remember that they do not have your best interest at heart because what they care about is making money and not your health.

Finally, you have the power to say "NO" by not buying these drinks – an effective way to stay away from them in the first place. When you are offered this sugar water to drink, please politely turn it down. When you turn down the drinks, you should ask for water instead. I say drink water because you cannot go wrong with drinking water.

Our bodies are made up of between sixty-five to seventy percent water, and water is what your body needs, not sugar water or even flavored water. What is wrong with drinking pure, clean, fresh water? Ours is a generation that has gone overboard with excesses because some do not drink water and think that it is something for them to be proud of. Water is what you need and nothing else. When you start putting pure water into your system, it will begin to flush and clean out all the junk and toxins in your system.

Your body is the temple of the Holy Spirit.

You may still be wondering why I am beating a dead horse. I have heard that something has to be said seven times for people to understand. This issue is so crucial that there is no problem repeating it.

Here is another reason, or the most compelling reason, you should watch what you put in your body. Those who do not yet have a personal relationship with Our Lord Jesus Christ may claim that they have total freedom and can do to their bodies as they seem fit. However, you who have been bought and redeemed by the blood of Jesus Christ know better, and you should not speak and act like those who are not under His authority.

Paul the Apostle had to address this issue of how to navigate through some thorny issues. In this case, he is dealing with adultery, where the brethren in Corinth felt that if their body wants something, they might as well have it. After all, it is just an act that involved the body, and after it is done, nothing happens. Paul was not buying into this idea at all, and this is what he told them:

> *"'I have the right to do anything,' you say—but not everything is beneficial. 'I have the right to do anything'—but I will not be mastered by anything.* You say, 'Food for the stomach and the stomach for food, and God will destroy them both.' The body, however, is not meant for sexual immorality but for the Lord, and the Lord for the body. By His power, God raised the Lord from the dead,*

and He will raise us also. **Do you not know that your bodies are members of Christ himself? Shall I then take the members of Christ and unite them with a prostitute? Never! Do you not know that he who unites himself with a prostitute is one with her in the body?** *For it is said, 'The two will become one flesh.' But whoever is united with the Lord is one with Him in spirit. Flee from sexual immorality. All other sins a person commits are outside the body, but whoever sins sexually, sins against their own body.* **Do you not know that your bodies are temples of the Holy Spirit, Who is in you, Whom you have received from God? You are not your own; you were bought at a price. Therefore, honor God with your bodies."** (1 Corinthians 6:12-20, NIV) (Note: emphases in bold are my own)

The common belief was that since the body was going to be destroyed eventually, it did not matter what it was used for. According to them, what got into the body was ultimately going to be destroyed since the body was not eternal. Therefore, committing adultery was not all that bad since it was strictly an act that involved the physical body. Likewise, food and drink were considered to be something that concerned just the body.

What these brethren had not realized is that things had changed, and the new had been ushered in. The people were still considering themselves to be separate from God and in charge of their bodies. But this was not the case. What Paul said concerning the body was revolutionary in that day. This was a time when God was living in temples. To say that God was now living in the human body was a big jump from this concept of God being confined in man-made edifices.

Our bodies do not belong to us. We are not our own; we cannot do as we please with our bodies because God owns them. While so much is spent taking care of physical buildings that we consider to be the house of God, many people neglect the true house of God, which is their body.

It is not acceptable to put junk in your physical house. In fact, any normal person cleans their house and makes sure that all the dirt is taken out and disposed of appropriately. After all, it is your dwelling place, and you do not want it to become infested with rats, cockroaches, and other pests. If you ever visit anybody and their house is not clean or is filled with waste, you are going to be uncomfortable. It will immediately strike you that something is out of order, and you will normally be uncomfortable in such an environment.

There is a great need for hygiene and sanitation in our dwelling places for obvious reasons, and all normal people take this seriously. Normal people understand this and make sure they adhere to it.

But when it comes to our bodies, it seems many forget that the body too needs to be cared for, both internally and externally. While it is easier for the external to be cleaned, oiled, and groomed nicely, it is more challenging to take care of the internal because our five senses drive this process.

We let things get into our bodies through our mouth, and this is driven by our taste buds, sight, and touch. This may not always be the case, but most of the time, the need for pleasure and to feel good is the main driver.

This explains why drinking something like sugar has such a strong hold on many people. Let's face it. Sugar is sweet and tastes well in the mouth. Imagine the taste of a cold, sweet beverage on a hot summer's day and how it makes you feel when you drink it. This soothing feeling that refreshes and makes you feel good is what drives you to come back for more and more.

The question of what drinking this sugar-loaded drink is doing to your body is thrown out of the window. Many do not even think about it. Even when the question pops up in their minds, the desire to satisfy that taste is stronger than the thought of what the sugar will do to their body. This explains why people keep drinking day in and day out, even though their waistline is increasing, and other things are going wrong in their bodies.

Your body should be treated with respect because it is the dwelling place of the Spirit of God. This is something that should make us excited! We are no longer commoners; we have become earthen containers that contain the Divine. Therefore, we cannot eat and drink just any-old-how. Watching what you eat and drink is the physical manifestation of your understanding that you are no longer your own and that your body has been bought at a price.

If you do not value it, you will not take care of it.

There is a misconception that anything to do with the body is less spiritual. Therefore, taking care of the body is less desirable. This misunderstanding is rooted in the false assumption that the body is earthly and tied to fleshy things, and there is nothing good in the flesh.

We are not the first generation to have such a low view of our bodies. From the two passages of scripture that we just read, it is very clear that the brethren in Corinth had the same problem. They did not consider their bodies to be worth much. If they did, they would not have been thinking of joining their bodies with those of prostitutes.

But Paul the Apostle's message to them was that something had changed fundamentally, and they better take note. Jesus died on the cross to not only redeem their souls but their bodies also. This is not refuting the fact that the body is perishing and will eventually decay but stating that it has become an instrument through which God does His work here on earth.

In other words, your body has become an essential tool in the hand of God. Your body is so valuable that God's only Son, Our Lord Jesus Christ, had to die on the cross for you. God, who created you, said everything He created is good. This implies that your body is good. In fact, it is good enough that the Holy Spirit now dwells in you.

What God says is valuable and must be valued by you. This starts with you understanding how your body works and how to take good care of it. One way to take care of the body is to watch what you put in your body. In our case, processed sugar is one of those things that are not healthy for the body and should be avoided at all costs.

Without a body, you are earthly-useless.

What can you do on Earth without a body? Is death not the separation of the spirit from the body? This implies that we earn the right to function in the earthly realm because we have a body. Without a body, we lose the right to be here. This is why we must take good care of our bodies. It is the only body that you have, and your mission on Earth is going to be accomplished through this body. Therefore, it is in your best interest to take care of your body.

God reaches those around us by using our bodies. We proclaim the good news of the Gospel through our mouths. We show acts of kindness by our actions. This may require using our hands to give something to somebody in need. At times we may have to use our feet to move from one place to another to do good for other people. The body is an integral part of our walk with God, and we should take good care of it.

As long as you are living on Earth, you have to do all within your power to be a good steward of your body, money, and all the other resources that God has given to us that make our lives on Earth possible.

Therefore, knowingly putting any substances into your body that will compromise the optimal functioning of your body is being unwise. You have the spirit of God living inside of you. The spirit of God is the spirit of truth and wisdom. This implies that you should walk as a wise person. If you still think that drinking sugar water is a smart thing to do, you will only have yourself to blame when payback time comes. Because sooner or later you will start reaping what you are sowing. In the case of sugar, it will take time to bear the fruit of destruction, but it surely will bear that fruit.

Your way of escape:

You can escape because there is much more to life than drinking sugar water. God has an important assignment for you, and you cannot do it if you are unhealthy. You might have been raised to drink sugar and eat sugar with impunity. Now you know better. For you to break away from this terrible addiction, you have to look at yourself squarely in the mirror and choose life over death.

Each time something is entering your mouth, you should evaluate if it is going to bring life to your body or death. Whatever you put in your mouth is going to somehow end up in your body. Therefore, you must eat carefully and ensure that you are not loading your body with sugar.

The way of escape for you lies in you taking charge of your own meals and controlling what goes into them. You may not like cooking, but that may be the only way you are going to break this sugar addiction. If you are always on the road and have no time to cook, you have to recognize the fact that without good health that traveling will stop sooner or later. Prioritizing your health is the only way to ensure that you stay on top of things. There must be zero tolerance when it comes to your health. If you don't already know, it will not hurt to remind you that your health is the most valuable resource that you have, and without it, nothing else matters.

Most people say that they understand their health is most important, yet their actions betray them. They make little or no effort to take care of their body. You can only mistreat and neglect your body for so long. Sooner or later, the neglect and abuse of the body will catch up with you, and it may be too late.

Now is the time to do something about it. Cut back on your sugar intake. Eliminate soda from your diet. When you go to the store, do not buy it. There are times I feel like drinking soda or anything sweet, and the only reason I do not drink is that it is nowhere to be found in our house. Do not say that you will buy it and keep it to entertain your visitors. Why would you give poison to your visitors and those that you love? If it is not good for you, it is not suitable for them either. Please don't serve soda and any other sugar-loaded drinks to those you love. You can never go wrong with water. This may sound like a harsh stance. Before you reject this suggestion, think about the devastation that diabetes, strokes, heart attacks, etc., have on the bodies of those who are impacted by these illnesses.

You are on a mission.

Do you know who you are and why you are here on Earth? When you ask many people who they are, they say they are a lawyer, accountant, teacher, pilot, geologist, professor, politician, etc. This is what they do, not who they are. When you discover who you are, why you are here, it will help you take a stand against sugar. You are going to do this because you know it will be unwise to allow sugar to sabotage this crucial mission. Talk is cheap, and knowledge without action will do you no good. The only way this book will be beneficial to you is if you taking some concrete action to cut out added sugar in what you eat and drink.

Here are a few things that can help you to break your sugar addiction:

Admit it.

Many addicts never get delivered because they are in denial. It is shocking to see somebody who is staggering and has slurred speech argue they are not drunk. No matter what those who are sober tell them, the drunk person will keep insisting that they are not drunk. Some even say that they have not tasted a single drop of alcohol. Yet their actions betray them.

You may still be thinking about why we have wasted so much ink and time writing about "innocent" sugar. Based on your personal judgment, you have concluded that the war against sugar can never be won. Let me put it this way. This book was not a war against the "global terror of sugar." It is a war on the terror sugar is posing to individuals. It is a call for you, as an individual, to take ownership of what goes into your body. If everybody else refuses to take care of what gets into their bodies, it does not matter. What matters the most is what you as an individual do.

A story is told about a man and his young son who were walking on the beach one cool evening. Suddenly they came across thousands of fish that a strong wave had washed up and abandoned on the beach. It was a pitiful sight, and the little boy became tearful. The task of putting back all the fish into the water was an enormous one. Darkness was fast approaching, and there was little or nothing the boy and his father could do to get the fish back into the water. With each passing second, thousands of fish were dying. Then the boy noticed that his father was doing something that did not make sense. Instead of scooping as many fish as possible and throwing them back into the water, his father would pick one single fish and throw it back into the water. This went on for a while. The boy was perplexed and confused. This prompted him to ask his father why he was throwing back some fish and allowing thousands to die. The boy wondered what difference it made if a few fish were saved. His father told him that it made a big difference to each fish that gets back into the water because that one fish is safe and will have an opportunity to reproduce. While it made no difference to the thousands that were dying, it was a hundred percent life for each fish that got back into the water.

The goal is not to save the whole world. For me and my house, we are soda-free and have been for over a decade now. We do not drink or buy. This is a huge thing for us. We are a lost customer to the soda, punch, and other sugary drink companies. Their advertisements do not work, and whatever campaigns they do to get us to buy their products falls on deaf ears. We do not need the government to regulate the size of the soda cups, because we have already chosen size zero!

You, too, can permanently defeat this monster. It is about you and nobody else. Let us win this war, one family at a time. But you must admit that you need help if you want to break free.

It is a battle.

You are going to have to fight to gain your freedom because sugar is not going to surrender without a fight. One way to fight is to be transformed by the renewal of your mind. This implies that you have to teach your mind about the dangers of sugar and the benefits of a processed-sugar-free life. Don't say that your grandfathers drank and ate sugary stuff all their lives and lived up to ninety before dying. You are not your grandfather, and times have changed. Their lifestyles were very different from ours.

It is going to be a fight at home and out of the house. The pressure to fit in and be like everyone else is going to be mounted against you. People who have tried to fight this battle and failed will not want you to succeed. Because if you do, you will make them look bad. They are going to accuse you of showing off and trying to make a big deal out of nothing. Don't listen to them. Don't eat poison to please other people.

Whatever you eat and drink is going into your body and not theirs.

You will find yourself in parties where everybody is drinking sugar, and the pressure to fit in will be intense. What you should do is to determine beforehand that water is good for you. When you get there, stick to the plan. Don't allow the pressure to please your host make you poison your body. Ask for water and drink water. At the end of the day, it is your body and your responsibility to take care of it.

Don't buy sugary drinks.

Out-of-sight is out-of-mind. If you do not take the soda home, there will be no soda to drink when you get thirsty at home. While this may sound so simple, many people fail because they think willpower will save them when they are tempted. The sad thing is that willpower does not always work. The best way to win is by not having any soda at home. You should adopt a zero-tolerance policy; if you do not buy soda and take it home, you have already won. But keeping soda at home and hoping that you will not drink it is like setting your clothes on fire and hoping that you will not get hurt. The last thing you want is to have a cold can of soda sitting in your refrigerator on a hot summer's evening. When those cravings for sugar hit, you do not want to be around soda. This is the point where many people yield, but one of the best ways to fight temptation is by removing it completely.

Somebody said that if they buy and keep the soda at home, it will not cause them to drink. Did you get that? They buy the soda and keep it at home so that the cravings will go away. This is backward thinking. If you have soda at home, the probability that you will drink is extremely high. But if you do not have the soda at home when the cravings hit you, there is nothing to drink, and you will not drink.

It is your life

Just because other people are drinking sugar and it is readily available does not mean that you should. It is your life and your health, and this is more important than anything else. If you are healthy and strong, you are going to be able to fulfill your destiny. This is something that you should take seriously enough to make the necessary changes that will enable you to be at your peak performance. Don't mortgage your future on the altar of soda and sugary drinks. You can never go wrong with water. The more water you drink, the better it is for your waistline and overall health.

Thank you for reading this book to the end. I am going to stop here by saying, Let those who have ears, hear.

This book was about sugary drinks and the dangers they pose. The assumption is that you are a child of God. But I may be mistaken. That is why the next chapter was included to help you learn how to become a child of God. My main motivator is the fact that your spiritual life is far more critical than the physical one. You are going to live forever, and now is the time to prepare for eternity. As somebody who has a holistic approach to life, I would be doing you a disservice if I didn't mention the most important aspect of your life—your spiritual life.

Turn to the next chapter and let us conclude this journey with what truly matters: your relationship with God and the eternal destiny of your soul.

Chapter 7
An eternal perspective is the ultimate one

---

*"For what profit is it to a man if he gains
the whole world, and loses his own soul?
Or what will a man give in exchange for his
soul?"*

– (Matthew 16:26, *NKJV*)

Congratulations! You have done what many people do not. Most people start books and never finish reading them. Yet you persevered, and now you are here.

There is nothing more important than being a child of God. I would be wicked if I did not share this truth with you. It is one of the most important things that you will ever do. It is more important than taking care of your physical body because your body will eventually decay. While you mustn't damage your body through drinking sugar, your body will eventually die. But there is a part of you that is more important. This is your spirit because it is eternal. Therefore, you must take care of your spirit.

I do not know where you are in your spiritual journey. No matter where you are, I strongly encourage you to read this chapter reflectively and make sure that you put things right with God. You are being offered an opportunity to have God come and live in you. This should excite you more than having the perfect body.

When Our Lord Jesus Christ says something, it is important that we take it seriously. Here is one of the most famous Bible verses that puts everything in perspective:

> *"For what profit is it to a man if he gains the whole world, and loses his own soul? Or what will a man give in exchange for his soul?"* (Matthew 16:26, NKJV)

Here Jesus Christ is asking a profound question that everybody must answer. You cannot afford to keep going through life without answering these questions because how your life ends will determine the answer to these questions. Interestingly, the body is not mentioned in this verse. But the soul is what is front and center because the body will finally die and decay, but the soul is going to live forever.

There is nothing more important than your soul, and you should take this seriously. While there is nothing wrong with being successful in this life, if you neglect what is more important, you are going to have all eternity to regret it.

The major assumption that has been throughout this book is that you are a believer in the Lord Jesus Christ. This implies that you have given your life to Him and accepted Him as your Lord and Savior. In addition to being born again, you are walking daily with the Lord and bearing the fruit of the Holy Spirit.

Having an eternal perspective is the ultimate goal because, at the end of the day, it is the eternal that matters. People have looked for the fountain of youth over the ages, and there is a lot of research right now to understand aging and how to reverse it. Even if we were to find the fountain of youth and drink from it so that we remain young forever, life on Earth would still have a lot of changes for us. This is because, even with reversing aging and making sure that we remain young here on Earth, we still have to face many other challenges as we live in a fallen world with many different problems.

I say all this to emphasize the importance of looking forward to our true and final home, where we will be with our Heavenly Father forever and ever. While life on earth is great, life in heaven is going to be greater and more fulfilling. This is something that all of God's children have to look forward to.

But if you are not yet a child of God, here is your opportunity to learn how to become one.

Follow instructions that will give you eternal life.

Life does not end when you die. There is an afterlife, and I am going to use this opportunity to tell you about it. Talking about the afterlife is not an indirect way for you to disengage with the present life, but a motivation for you to make the most of your time on Earth. While there are many arguments about which roads lead to God and which God is true, I am not going to dwell on these issues. The reason being that there is not enough room for us to do a comparative study of world religions.

That said, it is essential to note that while popular culture classifies Christianity as a religion and tries to compare it to other religions, the truth is that Christianity is not a religion. Religion is humanity trying to reach out to God; Christianity is the exact opposite, because God is reaching out to humanity and doing all to redeem us. To enjoy this redemption that God is offering you, must follow instructions.

I am writing this with the assumption that you have been reconciled to God and have a relationship with Him. If you do not yet have a relationship with God, I am going to give you the opportunity here to take care of that. This is one of the most important decisions you will ever make and should not be taken lightly. I do not want you to allow the failures of other believers that you might have interacted with to prevent you from getting into a personal relationship with your Heavenly Father. He has been waiting for you to come home and be reunited with Him.

Here is your opportunity to come home to the fullness of life and abundant life. All that you need and desire is in God, and you will never be forsaken or abandoned.

Let me start by asking you the following question. Do you have a personal relationship with Jesus Christ? This question is being asked because, although all roads lead to Rome, not all roads lead to the God of the Bible. Jesus Christ, who is God incarnate, made some exclusive claims when He said:

> *"Jesus answered, 'I am the way and the truth and the life. No one comes to the Father except through me.'"* (John 14:6, NIV)

This is a bold claim, and Jesus Christ died for standing up for this. He is simply saying that if you want a relationship with the God of the Bible, who is also the creator of heaven and earth, you must pass through Him. If you are not yet a follower of Jesus Christ, here is your opportunity to do so. I suggest this because it is going to get you connected to the source of all things. You will become spiritually alive and will live forever in the presence of God. Raising your child with the fear of God is the best thing you can do for you and your child.

The first and most important thing to understand is that we have all sinned. In other words, we cannot meet God's perfect standard, no matter how hard we try. Have you tried on your own to be good and realized many times how you do not measure up? Do you struggle with a void in your heart that nothing has been able to fill, no matter how hard you have tried? Are you comparing yourself to others and feeling that you are good because you are better than other people? If you answered yes to any of these questions, you need to understand that all of us have sinned, as the following scriptures clearly spell out:

"For all have sinned and come short of the glory of God." (Romans 3:23)

"For there is not a just man upon earth, that doeth good, and sinneth not." (Ecclesiastes 7:20)

"But we are all as an unclean thing, and all our righteousness as filthy rags, and we all do fade as a leaf; and our iniquities, like the wind, have taken us away." (Isaiah 64:6)

"As it is written, 'There is none righteous, no, not one.'" (Romans 3:10)

"For whosoever shall keep the whole law, and yet offend in one point, he is guilty of all." (James 2:10)

"If we say that we have no sin, we deceive ourselves, and the truth is not in us." (1 John 1:8)

We have all sinned and need God's forgiveness. This is the place to start. When you acknowledge this, then you will be able to receive God's free forgiveness and salvation.

The third crucial thing to understand is the devastating consequences of sin. You may be wondering why sin is such a bad thing and why we are making such a big deal about it. Everybody, including you, should be concerned about the consequences of sin because, according to the following verses, sin has a wage, and that wage is death:

> *"For the wages of sin is death, but the free gift of God is eternal life in Christ Jesus our Lord."* (Romans 6:23, ESV)

> *"Therefore, just as sin came into the world through one man, and death through sin, and so death spread to all men because all sinned."* (Romans 5:12, ESV)

> *"But as for the cowardly, the faithless, the detestable, as for murderers, the sexually immoral, sorcerers, idolaters, and all liars, their portion will be in the lake that burns with fire and sulfur, which is the second death."* (Revelation 21:8, ESV)

This death is both physical and spiritual. Sin can cause us to die in this life, and if we die in sin, we will be separated from God forever. You do not want this to happen to you and your child or children; you want to be able to live forever in the presence of God. This is why the second crucial thing to think about is the wages of sin.

The fourth crucial step is to ask God to forgive your sins. The good news is that God has already made provision to forgive our sins and is ready and willing to forgive us all our sins. As you will soon discover, God has already made the first move.

"For God so loved the world, that he gave his only begotten Son, that whosoever believeth in him should not perish, but have everlasting life." (John 3:16)

"Jesus said unto her, 'I am the resurrection, and the life: he that believeth in me, though he were dead, yet shall he live: And whosoever liveth and believeth in me shall never die. Believest thou this?'" (John 11:25-26)

"And they said, 'Believe on the Lord Jesus Christ, and thou shalt be saved, and thy house.'" (Acts 16:31)

"That if thou shalt confess with thy mouth the Lord Jesus, and shalt believe in thine heart that God hath raised him from the dead, thou shalt be saved. For with the heart man believeth unto righteousness, and with the mouth confession is made unto salvation." (Romans 10:9-10)

"Whosoever believeth that Jesus is the Christ is born of God: and every one that loveth Him that begat loveth Him also that is begotten of Him." (1 John 5:1)

Now that you have confessed and asked Jesus to forgive your sins, your sins have been forgiven and will be remembered no more.

The fifth and final thing to do is invite Jesus into your heart. Now is your opportunity to surrender your life to Jesus and invite Him to come into your heart. Jesus will never force Himself on anyone. He is outside, according to the following scriptures, knocking and waiting for you to invite Him to come in:

> *"Behold, I stand at the door, and knock: if any man hear my voice, and open the door, I will come in to him, and will sup with him, and he with Me."* (Revelation 3:20)

> *"But as many as received Him, to them gave He power to become the sons of God, even to them that believe on His name."* (John 1:12)

> *"And because ye are sons, God hath sent forth the Spirit of His Son into your hearts, crying, Abba, Father."* (Galatians 4:6)

> *"That Christ may dwell in your hearts by faith; that ye, being rooted and grounded in love."* (Ephesians 3:17)

Jesus Christ is waiting for you to invite Him to come in, and you can do that by praying and asking Him to do so. Use your own words to talk to Him or use the following words, called "The Sinner's Prayer" (by John Barnett).

The following prayer expresses the desire to transfer trust to Christ alone for eternal salvation. If its words speak of your own heart's desire, praying them can be the link that will connect you to God.

"Dear God, I know that I am a sinner, and there is nothing that I can do to save myself. I confess my complete helplessness to forgive my own sin or to work my way to heaven. At this moment, I trust Christ alone as the One who bore my sin when He died on the cross. I believe that He did all that will ever be necessary for me to stand in Your holy presence. I thank you that Christ was raised from the dead as a guarantee of my own resurrection. As best as I can, I now transfer my trust to Him. I am grateful that He has promised to receive me despite my many sins and failures. Father, I take you at your word. I thank you that I can face death now that You are my Savior. Thank You for the assurance that You will walk with me through the deep valley. Thank you for hearing this prayer. In Jesus' Name, Amen."

Praise God, hallelujah! If you just said this prayer, I am super excited for you and want to use this opportunity to welcome you into the kingdom of God and God's family. This is one of the most critical decisions you will ever make because it has eternal consequences. You are now a newborn baby in Christ and need spiritual nourishment to grow in your faith. If you need more information on what to do next, send an email.

Please, you must understand the fundamental nature of this decision you have just made. I want to highlight the fact that the focus has not been for you to join a religion or to become religious. Religion is man seeking to please God. But here we have presented a picture of God seeking man. God loved the entire world and gave His son to pay the penalty for our sins. This point is being made so that you understand that you are being called into a personal relationship with Jesus - not just some religious observances. While church membership is essential, it is more important that you establish a healthy and vibrant relationship with Jesus Christ.

Resources for your new walk with God:

Our lives on Earth pale in comparison to eternity. There is no comparison at all because eternity has no measure. Even if you live to be more than 100 years old on Earth, you will not make it to 200; your life on this side has a limit. Therefore, the best thing to do is to factor eternity into the equation of your life.

This is what you have just done, and I applaud you for that. Now that you have become a child of God, you need to learn how to walk with Him. You need to learn how to love God and know Him.

When we love somebody, we spend time with them, talk to them and get to know them. This is not done in a day, but it takes time. You just started this relationship with your Heavenly Father, and you have to learn how to know Him and grow in intimacy with Him. If you need resources on what to do, here is the best way to contact us: eternalkingdom101@gmail.com

Acknowledgement

I will start by thanking God for opening my eyes to the dangers of sugar. I can say that it has taken divine intervention for me to be where I am right now. The call of God upon my life and the mission He has for me makes it imperative for me to live a holistic, healthy life. I need a strong and well-functioning body to take the inspirational message of hope across the globe. I keep telling my wife that God is up to something - our lives are so important that we cannot just waste them through what we eat and drink.

Special thanks to my wife, who led the war against sugar in our home and our lives. Her #sugarsucks campaign is part of the reason this book has come to fruition, as she is the person who went cold turkey in our house as far as soda is concerned. We have caught up with her. It was not easy, but her persistence and consistency made it possible for us to step up and step out.

The work reported in this book is not entirely mine, and I want to thank all those who have worked and are still working tirelessly to expose the dangers of sugar.

To all my fans who read my books, write reviews, and send in words of encouragement: without your continuous support, this work would not have been possible. Your words of encouragement keep me going.

The editorial team has done a phenomenal job in turning my sometimes disjointed thoughts into something legible. Thank you so much for all you do. The diligence of the design team of IEM Press has made this book possible; thank you for everything.

About the Author

Dr. Eric Tangumonkem was born and raised in a caldera on the Cameroon Volcanic Line in Cameroon, West Africa. He has a bachelor's degree in Geology and a minor in Sociology from the University of Buea in Cameroon, a Master's in Earth Sciences from the University of Yaounde in Cameroon, and a Doctorate in Geosciences from the University of Texas at Dallas. In addition to being a geoscientist with extensive experience in the oil and gas industry, he is a teacher and an entrepreneur. Currently, he teaches at Embry Riddle Aeronautical University, and West Hills College. He is also the President of IEM Approach, a premier personal growth and leadership development company based on the infinite wisdom revealed over the ages. He is on a mission to inspire, equip, and motivate people from all walks of life to find their God-given purpose, and to pursue and possess it. He is married and has five children.

Available for speaking engagements:

If you want to invite Dr. Tangumonkem to come and speak, you can call him at 317-975-0806, or email him at eternalkingdom101@gmail.com.

Available for speaking engagements:

If you want to invite Dr. Tangumonkem to come and speak, you can call him using this number 214-908-3963 or email him at eternalkingdom101@gmail.com

Here are his social media handles:

https://www.erictangumonkem.com

https://www.linkedin.com/in/drtangumonkem/

https://twitter.com/DrTangumonkem

https://www.facebook.com/drtangumonkem

tangumonkem.tumblr.com

https://instagram.com/tangumonkem/

http://www.pinterest.com/erictangumonkem/

https://vimeo.com/user23079930

https://www.youtube.com/c/EricTangumonkem

Other Resources by the Author

Coming to America: A Journey of Faith

Do you struggle with trusting God with your finances? Feel that God is calling you to do something big but you can't see how it will be accomplished? Fear that He has abandoned you after starting your journey of faith? Coming to America: A Journey of Faith is Eric Tangumonkem's story of wrestling with these thoughts and doubts. God called him to America from Cameroon to pursue graduate studies at the University of Texas at Dallas, but he had no money to put towards this dream. In this book, Tangumonkem shares his journey of learning to trust God as he stepped out in faith and came to America despite a lack of funds. He also shares some of his formative experiences prior to this call-experiences that will encourage readers in their faith. Tangumonkem's life is a testimony to the faithfulness of God, and he is careful to give Him all of the glory.

https://www.amazon.com/dp/B082D16PD5/ref=cm_sw_r_tw_dp_x_RXTmFbKTVRZCR via @amazon

The Use and Abuse of Titles in The Church

This book examines reasons behind the disturbing proliferation of titles in Christendom in recent times by seven distinguished Christian professionals. The book challenges readers to stay on the straight and narrow road, which celebrates ministers with titles bestowed based on sound Biblical foundations, while shunning those with titles associated with self-promotion and doctrinal errors. The book also provides the following actionable insights:· How to identify the proper use of titles · A history on the use of titles in Christendom How to avoid the pitfalls of acquiring bogus titles An understanding of the relationship between titles and leadership

https://www.amazon.com/dp/B01E5H36CC/ref=cm_sw_r_tw_dp_x_b4TmFb2K22RPE via @amazon

Seven Success Keys Learned From My Father

This is a book about my father, my teacher, my role model and hero. A man of passion like any other man, but a man of exceptional qualities and abilities as well. The following are the seven keys to success my father passed to me: Fear of God, Humility, Education, Integrity, Hard work, Prayer and Vision. All these keys have been instrumental in making me who I am today. In addition to these keys, my father was present when we were growing up. He made it a point of duty to talk the talk and walk the walk before us. This book illustrates how these seven keys to success were interwoven in our day-to-day lives and how they have opened unprecedented doors of success to me. My sincere prayer for you as you read this book is that these keys will open all doors for you and bring the success you desire so strongly. Amen!

https://www.amazon.com/dp/B01N0A0YYC/ref=cm_sw_r_tw_dp_x_I6TmFbP3QSX91 via @amazon

Viajando a América: Un Camino de Fe (Spanish Edition)

¿Lucha con confiar en Dios con sus finanzas? Siente que Dios le está llamando a hacer algo grande, pero usted no puede ver la forma en que se llevará a cabo? ¿Teme a que Él le ha abandonado después de comenzar su camino de fe?

Viajando a América: Un Camino de Fe es la historia de Eric Tangumonkem, de su lucha con estos pensamientos y dudas. Dios lo llamó a América desde Camerún para realizar estudios de posgrado en la Universidad de Texas en Dallas, pero no tenía dinero para seguir este llamado. En este libro, Tangumonkem comparte su viaje de aprender a confiar en Dios cuando caminó en la fe y llegó a Estados Unidos a pesar de su falta de fondos. También comparte algunas de sus experiencias formativas previas a esta convocatoria-experiencias que estimularán a los lectores en su fe. La vida de Tangumonkem es un testimonio de la fidelidad de Dios, y él tiene cuidado en darle toda la.

https://www.amazon.com/dp/B018H9S2BY/ref=cm_sw_r_tw_dp_x_hdUmFb8QN2148 via @amazon

MON ODYSSÉS AMÉRICAINE: UNE EXPÉRIENCE DE FOI (French Edition)

As-tu du mal à confier tes soucis financiers au Seigneur? Ressens-tu que Dieu t'appelle à faire quelque chose de grand, mais tu ne sais comment cela va se réaliser? Crains-tu qu'il va t'abandonner en chemin? Mon Odyssée Américaine: une expérience de foi est l'histoire d'Éric Tangumonkem et de sa lutte contre le doute et les pensées susmentionnées. Dieu l'a appelé depuis le Cameroun pour aller poursuivre ses études supérieures à l'Université du Texas à Dallas, mais il n'avait pas d'argent pour réaliser ce rêve. Dans ce livre, le Dr Tangumonkem partage avec vous les péripéties de son voyage qui l'ont amené à faire davantage confiance à Dieu alors qu'il se rendit aux États-Unis par la foi. Il partage également certaines des expériences qui l'ont bâti avant même son appel –expériences qui vont encourager les lecteurs dans leur foi. La vie du Dr Tangumonkem est un témoignage de la fidélité de Dieu à qui il rend toute la gloire.

https://www.amazon.com/dp/B00T7XBPMS/ref=cm_sw_r_tw_dp_x_heUmFbZH8NZWN via @amazon

God's Supernatural Agenda: 7 Secrets to Lasting Wealth and Prosperity

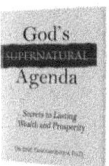

Is there something more valuable than money, precious stones, silver, and gold? Do you desire to be wealthy and prosperous? Are you already wealthy and prosperous, yet you feel empty and unsatisfied? Are you uncomfortable talking about money because it is "the root of all evil"? This book will not present shortcuts or get-rich-quick schemes, but important principles, laws, and processes involved in generating lasting wealth.

You see, God desires for ALL of us to prosper today and for all eternity. He has a divine reason for that desire, and He has given us the way to attain it. God's Supernatural Agenda: 7 Secrets to Lasting Wealth and Prosperity presents His blueprint for prosperity and explains why it is what truly matters.

https://www.amazon.com/dp/B07WJLB4BM/ref=cm_sw_r_tw_dp_x_QfUmFb11KQQN0 via @amazon

Racism, Where Is Your Sting?
A provocative look at the beginning and the end of racism

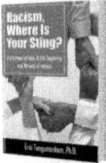

Each time the issue of racism is mentioned, tensions immediately run high, reason is thrown out the window, and emotional outbursts run rampant. Even though a lot of effort has been done to fight it, the devastating consequences continue to this day.

In this book, Dr. Tangumonkem challenges the status quo and presents a perspective that is both provocative and inspirational. Contrary to what you hear from those stoking the flames of racism and fermenting hate and bigotry, we are not at the mercy of racism. In fact, he dives deep into history to explain why the tendency to be racist is present in each one of us, regardless of skin color. The good news is that the victory has already been won — all we need is to live it out. When we stare right at this supercharged issue with fresh, unfiltered eyes, a seismic shift happens. Perhaps, the light at the end of racism is in sight.

https://www.amazon.com/dp/B082D16PD5/ref=cm_sw_r_tw_dp_x_4gUmFbRFX7EQQ via @amazon

The Intersection of Faith, Migration and God's Mission:
A call for the people of God in the West to engage in Mission Dei

"Our missionary brothers, sisters, sons, daughters, husbands, and wives would travel thousands of miles to share the gospel to people in faraway lands. They are willing to sacrifice all to share the love of God with these people. Times are changing. Now, God is bringing people from foreign lands right to our shores. Is this a new mission? What is His reason? Unfortunately, the present political climate and rhetoric are making it extremely difficult, if not impossible, for us to have a level-headed discussion when it comes to this topic of migration. It seems the people of God are divided on what to do as well. We have been tasked to be the light of the world. We cannot hide behind nationalistic tendencies or political correctness. We must stand up and be the light in a time of darkness. We must speak the truth in love in a time of fear. We must advocate for peace in a time of hatred."

https://www.amazon.com/dp/B083P5QCW1/ref=cm_sw_r_tw_dp_x_8lUmFbYSP3NR4 via @amazon

Phones, Electronic Devices, and You: Who Is in Charge?

Do you have a serious fear of missing out (FOMO) when you're not online?•Do you have separation anxiety when you don't have your phone with you?•Do you text while driving? •Are your electronic devices on 24/7?If you or someone you know experience these things, read on. It is true that our phones and electronic devices have become part-and-parcel of our lives. It is connecting us in ways unimaginable. Unfortunately, it is also causing a lot of havoc in our relationships because one cannot have meaningful connections with somebody and be on the phone at the same time. This book was written to help you put your phone and electronic devices in the right place, especially when it comes to your interactions with other people. Your world will not crumble if you go offline at the appropriate times. Whose life and relationships are at stake? Yours. Take charge.

https://www.amazon.com/dp/B083P4YHRR/ref=cm_sw_r_tw_dp_x_VmUmFbT4TYCD5 via @amazon

How to Inspire Your Online student: 7 Steps to Achieving Unparalleled Success in An E-Learning Environment

Online teaching and learning are here to stay. We are living in an exciting time, with the opportunity to educate the world at our fingertips. This book makes a case for the need to bring inspiration in the online learning environment, and it explores how far this can go to raise a new generation of students who will have a local and global impact.

The flexibility, versatility, and dynamic nature of online learning holds the key to arriving at global solutions that have a regional signature. While students from all over the world are connected to world-class professors from around the globe, they will be able to receive customized solutions to meet the needs of their individual communities.

While some countries can afford the rising costs of education, others cannot. Even the countries that can afford to educate their citizens are experiencing ever-increasing expenses; one way to cut those costs without compromising quality is through online delivery.

This book explains why and how this is possible and how you, as an online instructor, can play a vital role.

https://www.amazon.com/dp/B08G5BY56D/ref=cm_sw_r_tw_dp x y7.qFbTME9W4Q via @amazon

How to succeed as an online student: 7 Secrets to excelling as an online student

How do you know if you have what it takes to study and succeed online? From what I have observed, there is a large chasm between "knowing" and "doing." If knowing was all that was necessary to be successful, all of us would be hugely successful.

Fortunately, this book is designed in such a way that it will move you from knowing to doing. Therefore, you should make up your mind to act on the information presented in this book. Without a concerted effort to apply this information, the secrets will not work. The challenge for you might be making the necessary changes to be successful. I hope that this resource will help you succeed in your online courses.

https://www.amazon.com/dp/B08G5BY56D/ref=cm_sw_r_tw_dp_x_qE9vFbXB0ZKAQ via @amazon

Welcome to America: 52 Proven Strategies That Will Position You to Excel as an Immigrant

You are thousands of miles away from your country of birth and will need to learn new skills to adapt to this new culture. You are one among millions who have landed on the shores of this great country in pursuit of "The American Dream."

Your success depends heavily on what you do during your first couple of years here.

When I arrived in the US, there was no book like this to give me a springboard to move at the speed of light. That is why this book was written: to help you succeed in a big way.

You have been presented with an opportunity to reinvent yourself, and this process will be directed and implemented by you and nobody else. You will receive much help along the way if you are courageous enough to ask. Besides support from others, you should learn from the get-go that you are the ultimate driver of your boat. How fast you go and how far you reach is up to you. Unlike where you have come from, here, you are expected to take charge and be responsible for your own outcome.

You have sacrificed a great deal to be in the US, and there is no turning back or room for failure. All you must do is follow the time-tested advice you are about to receive; believe it, speak it, act on it, and you will be unstoppable.

The 52 strategies listed in the book are not just for the immigrants who migrate to the United States of America, but for all who migrate within or out of the country and for those with whom the immigrants will be interacting. This is an attempt to maximize the potential that migration brings and lessen the downside that is associated with it.This book presents a holistic approach to health, wealth, and fitness; the physical and spiritual must be in synergy for real, lasting, and sustainable success.

To Exercise or Not to Exercise: The Connection Between Bodily Exercise and Spirituality

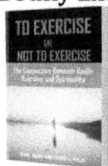

"I was given a job and given a horse to get the job done. I overworked my horse; it died, and now I cannot do my job."

This is a story that has influenced me profoundly and spurred this book.

Your body is the horse. Are you taking good care of it? Now is the best time to look after your health; your productivity depends on it.

What is the one thing that will negatively impact your productivity? No matter how talented you are and how lofty your goals, without good health, nothing else matters. While many take their health for granted and assume, they can afford to neglect it, the fact is that they cannot. The cost of ill health is so high, none of us can afford it.

This book presents a holistic approach to health, wealth, and fitness; the physical and spiritual must be in synergy for real, lasting, and sustainable success.

IEM PRESS

To order additional copies of this book call:
214-908-3963
Or visit our website at
www.iempublishing.com

If you enjoyed this quality
custom-published book,
drop by our website for more
books and information.

*"Inspiring, equipping, and motivating
one author at a time."*

www.ingramcontent.com/pod-product-compliance
Lightning Source LLC
Chambersburg PA
CBHW071551040426
42452CB00008B/1132